Churches and How They Grow

M. WENDELL BELEW

Churches and How They Grow

BROADMAN PRESS
Nashville, Tennessee

ISBN: 0-8054-2522-5
4225-22

Library of Congress Catalog Card Number: 79–157402
Dewey Decimal Classification: 254
Printed in the United States of America
5.F7118

a dedication

to

Edna, Wendell, Cathy, Belle

CONTENTS

IN THE BEGINNING

"Today I will find Carthage," I thought, as I went to the open window of my quarters and looked out at the place which was strange to me, Bizerte, Tunisia, North Africa. On the far side of a canal an Arab was leading a camel. The bright morning sun pinpointed a blooming rose bush against the side of a pastel wall. Hills changed through blue to yellow ochre. Bougainvillea mottled drab surroundings with staccato outbursts of color.

Hurriedly I dressed and proceeded to find a car for the quest I would make alone. My limited knowledge of the history of the Christian church had implanted two names firmly in mind, Cyprian and Tertullian, early pastors of the church in Carthage, that ancient citadel-city which had been an outpost of civilization and Christianity for five hundred years after Christ. I would find it.

The map which I had obtained barely marked the place and the road I chose was shell-pocked by Allied bombings. Rommel's forces had recently been driven from N. Africa and equipment and quickly marked graves attested to the fact that it had been a major thoroughfare of war.

Numerous byways were encountered and my uncertainties grew until I encountered the ruin of an ancient aqueduct. Could it have brought water to my quested city? My course had been westerly and the aqueduct ran north and south. I turned left beneath a remnant arch and followed the new route, now going east until I came to the crest of a hill. Below lay the evidence of a once-proud city. Beyond, the azure of the Mediterranean.

I parked the car in the shade of a fragmented arch. For a moment I surveyed the scene and sought my memory for what had transpired here. My commemoration was shattered by a "Hey, Joe, wanna see the city?"

An inevitable little Arab boy had appeared from nowhere to serve as tour guide, first cousin to the Bizerte type, with the "Hey, Joe, wanna shine your shoes?"

IN THE BEGINNING

"Today I will find Carthage," I thought, as I went to the open window of my quarters and looked out at the place which was strange to me, Bizerte, Tunisia, North Africa. On the far side of a canal an Arab was leading a camel. The bright morning sun pinioned a blooming rose bush against the side of a pastel wall. Hills shaded through blue to yellow ochre. Bougainvillea startled drab surroundings with staccato outbursts of color.

Hurriedly I dressed and proceeded to find a car for the trip I would make alone. My limited knowledge of the history of the Christian church had implanted two names firmly in mind; Cyprian and Tertullian, early pastors of the church at Carthage, that ancient citadel-city which had been an outpost of civilization and Christianity for five hundred years after Christ. I would find it.

The map which I had obtained barely marked the place and the road I chose was shell-pocked by Allied bombings. Rommel's forces had recently been driven from it. Abandoned equipment and quickly marked graves attested to the fact that it had been a major thoroughfare of war.

Numerous byways were encountered and my uncertainties grew until I encountered the ruin of an ancient aqueduct. Could it have brought water to my quested city? My course had been westerly and the aqueduct ran north and south. I turned left beneath a remnant arch and followed the now here, now gone, ruin until I came to the crest of a hill. Below lay the evidence of a once-proud city. Beyond, the azure of the Mediterranean.

I parked the car in the shade of a fragmented arch. For a moment I surveyed the scene and sought my memory for what had transpired here. My commemoration was shattered by a "Hey, Joe, wanna see the city?"

An inevitable little Arab boy had appeared from nowhere to serve as tour guide, first cousin to the Bizerte type, with his, "Hey Joe, wanna shine your shoes?"

My knowledge of his language was diminutive. His of mine had probably already been revealed. No, I would go it alone, assuring myself that I did not really resent parting with the coins which his services would demand. I wanted simply to be alone, unhurried by a competitive will which might place a greater importance on what it might think important to my knowledge.

He followed slowly, kicking stones from the dusty path, venting his frustrations that a profession such as his was being shunned. I considered giving him a coin to buy my release to aloneness.

"Wanna see where the Christians were?" A new question was posed. His greater wisdom had found my search. His services were now indispensable to me. I had to have him as my guide lest after all this seeking I should miss *the place*.

The bargain was struck, completed.

With animation he poured out his Arabic descriptions, or vindications. If the latter, they at least were hidden in tonal qualities which seemed enlightening. Once, I think I heard "University of Michigan." He skipped me down the hill, across the giant stones of the outer wall.

"Whoa, now!"

Not waiting to discern if he understood my rural vernacular, I stopped. What giant stones! What prowess of engineering had contrived to get them there? Who had masterminded the building of the wall? And who had assured the populace that they were safe, secure behind it?

And that other force which tore it down?

Nature had played its part, but there was a time, a movement which engineered its destruction. Someone had contrived how it should be done. Some*one* had assured his followers that there was a way to break the wall, and led them to mount their catapults against the gates. Superior force and technology had won.

Down from the pile of rocks that had been a wall and through the periphery of the city we moved. My guide pointed to a cistern-like crypt and the ruins of a palace. Still, I did not understand what he said but his speech inflections were background to my assumptions.

Over outlines of villas, shops, and then, did he say "forum" and/or "praetorian"? There, in the center of the city stood the lonely vestiges of once-proud creations of the sculpted arts of man. Crowds had thronged the streets and had consulted here. And between the two imposing ruins crouched a gem of structural composition.

My guide needed not to explain but said, "See where the Christians were?"

Trance-like I moved to its interior. Frgaments of a mosaic floor . . . a baptistry, indented in the floor, with stone steps leading down and up . . . marble columns which once had supported a roof. Obviously, this house once had held a church.

Oblivious to the ruin and to my guide, I strained to hear the voices of those who had built the church and the house. When had they begun to speak? Perhaps a voyager disembarked upon the pier one day and his heart was filled to overflowing with the *truth*, newfound by him. And with that Divine imperative branded upon his life, he sought someone to tell.

Tell whom?

There was a man, a seller of perfumes, or silver, or of fish, who long had sought for *truth*. Grand force propelled the two together (the one who sought to tell and the one who sought to hear) and one said, "Wanna buy some ________?" The other said, "I have good news." Earnestly the two conversed together. Snatches of the conversation caught my ear, "Good News,". . . "unto us a child is born . . . unto us a Son is given . . . wonderful, counsellor, Prince of Peace . . . to heal the brokenhearted, feed the hungry, give abundant life."

Incredible that the two *hungers* should be so quickly satisfied. The *hunger* to tell and the *hunger* to hear. Psychologists might for millenniums consider the validity of the experiences but quickly now the two men hurry up the pier and disappear to an apartment above the shop. (Was it perhaps that very one there across the street?)

The *hearer* calls his wife and after but the briefest introduction the good news is related in the vernacular of the *new hearer*. He only now and then checks with his informer for verification. They are *three!*

Never would the church of Carthage exceed this time of greatness. There would be more in number but never would it be more "church" than now. And it would grow.

At first the good news would sweep the city like some contagion, the markets would fluctuate, the forum's dialogue would reflect the new *truth* and its implications. Economics, politics, and government would all become arrayed to test the metal of the *truth*. Devotees of each of the "sets" of ideas would form and reform to repulse (or accept) the challenge.

Polarization of the concepts of the world against that of the good news was soon accomplished. The *truth* was too radical to grant its promises and yet countenance "life as usual."

The little church was driven into hiding. Secretly it held its meetings (perhaps in that corner by the crypt or in the lee of the city wall). Its meetings were announced by whispered word or by that beauteous symbol of the early church, the fish, pressed on papyrus fragment, or clay tablet, or crudely drawn upon a door.

There were the years of sufferings by the church. Were they one century? Two? They were times in which the church growth was impeded. A plague hit the city and many, many people died. So many, in fact, that bodies were simply dumped outside the houses into the streets for it was thought that to touch the dead or dying was to incur death.

It was the pastor of the church and its members (whose faith removed their fear of dying) who worked to remove the dead for burial and who ministered to the sick. In its moments of compassion the city could not forget this evidence of ministry and of faith. In its moments of concern that its "way of life" was threatened by the Christian acts of faith it could not forget.

But there were times when the evil intent of people could not tolerate the good intent of the church. Perhaps there in the forum the judgment was pronounced. "The pastor must die!" was the verdict.

"He disturbed." "He sought for justice (or peace)" was the accusation. The world has never been able to bear much of the love done in the name of Christ.

Outside the city wall, in a place where once a forest stood, a scaffold was erected. Cyprian, pastor of the tiny church, who had sought things of the Kingdom, was to be executed. The executioner with axe was on hand. Who was he? The executioner? Why was it that just before the fatal blow Cyprian gave him *thirty pieces of silver*?

The pastor's head was severed from his body. Members of the congregation stepped forward and dipped their handkerchiefs in his blood. Folded them, and hid them within their garments. Nor, would they forget!

But for the years! (Were they enough to make a century? Two?) A rationale of coexistence began to be formed between those in the world and those who were "in the world but not of it." This began to be formed because those outside the church could not help but see the virtue of those within. They were sometimes kinsmen or long-time friends. It began because of the very concern which the Christian had for the lost and for peace. The Christian longed for a reconciliation.

Christianity became acceptable, even respectable. It began to reach some people of prominence in the city. The church no longer had to meet in secret. It may have even rented a store-front building, then a house. At its meetings it sang gospel songs, and the curious passersby might ask, "What's going on in there?" and the reply would come, "That's where the Christians are."

The church had a fervor. Because of its meaning to the well-being of the city, it was possible to perform a great openness in witnessing. As its members studied of the great meeting at Pentecost an evangelism committee may have suggested an open-air "revival" in the marketplace. Christianity was "in." Hordes of people joined the church. A new meeting house must be built to show the visitors to the city the regard in which Chrisianity was held.

A building committee was appointed and charged with the responsibility of finding the choicest site and erecting a building more beautiful than those temples of other gods.

The congregation was ecstatic with the report that due to the influence of some persons of the church a site had been obtained immediately by the forum and/or praetorian. Craftsmen volunteered their services, merchantmen offered to find and contribute choice marble from Greece. Artisans would give their all. What a spirit of fellowship and endeavor! Strangers from many lands would come to Carthage and note the edifice so conspicuously located and would ask, "What's that?" and any citizen of the city would reply, "That's where the Christians are."

What happened then? Each person who had participated in the building had given something of himself. A godly act! A Christian stewardship! Is it possible that a godly virtue can obscure a goal? That a utility can become an ultimate? That a house can become a church?

I do not seek to answer. I only know that an enemy came to Carthage and pitted its strength and technology against the city. The enemy broached the walls and made its destructive way to the center of the city and lay waste the forum and (or) praetorian and the house that was between.

For nearly fifteen hundred years the excitedly whispered "Good News" has been stilled about this place. In other places where Christians and the political system with which they are affiliated have been overrun by enemies and the enemies have become Christians.

But here? In Carthage?

My little Arab guide, devotee of Mohammed, who until now had left me to my reverie, smiled, or was that a sneer? and said,

"See Joe? See where the Christians were?"

Dry leaves blew and swirled through what had been a baptistry.

I long

would wonder why

some churches grow

and others die.

M. W. B.

1 Some Churches Grow—or Die

Some considerations about church growth

Church growth . . .

. . Is not easily defined

. . Implies numbers

. . Is relative

. . . to what is going on in the church community

. . . to what is going on within the fellowship of the church

. . . to time and place

. . May be associated with spurious evangelism

. . May be limited to cultivative witness

. . . or what the church does "far away"

. . . or what the preacher does behind the pulpit

. . . or what the church does "in the world"

Churches die

. . Because it is *easier* than living

. . Because it may appear "competitive"

. . Because the location of the house makes living impossible

. . Because they have served themselves so long their direction cannot be changed

. . Because the community has changed

Although much has been written about the growth of Christianity and the church as it has occurred historically, both inside and outside the United States, contemporarily, we are a bit confused as to what church growth is all about.

Church growth is not easily defined. The mere expression of the term sends proponents of their differing concepts scurrying to the fore with all the defensive weapons they can muster. Some would retire from the battle before it ever has begun with exclamations of disgust.

For our purposes here, we will deal with some factors which relate to growing churches in their local settings and, of course, this will have its bearing on the larger church.

Case studies have been made of a large number of churches which are growing. They represent several of the growing denominations in America today and are found in open country, rural, small towns, city and urban environments.

Certainly, growth implies numbers. Numbers are not "faddish" now as for some years there has been a rather violent aversion to their use as regards the church. Numbers, as relate to population explosion and billions of dollars spent on national defense, or salaries, or drug addicts are "in," but numbers as relate to the churches are "out." Without apology, we are interested in numbers. Not as a mere statistic to report a burgeoning church roll but to reflect an interest that it was not his will that "*one* should perish"; and that of the early church which reported that "*many were added to the church*." It was not Christ's will that the church would fail. In fact, he said it would not.

Our problem is not so much with counting, however, as to know *where* and *when* to *begin* counting. The Kingdom's growth is mighty and from within, like *leaven* it works until it has affected the whole. Its *influence* is felt upon the man *before* he becomes a citizen of the Kingdom. The church (its corporate and individual constituency) begins its growth as it brings to bear its influence upon those *outside*. This influence may not produce Christians for many years, yet again, it may produce quickly.

We recognize that to begin counting with the moment an individual says "I believe" is not always valid. Our churches have too many members who have said "I believe," and yet act as though they did not. To begin counting with the time the church *touched the lives* of people has its problems too. For the church has *touched the lives* of most everyone in the world. Our whole American society is permeated with the influences of Christianity but that has not made Christians of the whole populace. We do not have the final authority upon the count but surely we would not wish to give up on some measurement of church growth because we are confused with this. Political systems of America have some difficulty along this line as well. They do not have the final answer as to the number of adherents they have gained until the votes are cast and counted. They are not deterred however from trying to reach as *many* as possible.

It is incredible that many churchmen have almost abandoned a desire for church growth because they do not know how to *figure* it. To write off an adjacent church's phenomenal growth with the judgment that "they are only interested in numbers," or "they won't hold out" is rather judgmental.

Church growth is relative. It is relative to what is going on in the community in which it exists. It is relative to what is going on in the church itself. It is relative to the time and place in which church growth occurs.

A changing community affects the church. The community's image of what the church is or ought to be does as well. If the people of the community are moving away, the church may be "growing" even though its membership declines. Or, if many people are moving into the community the church may not be "growing" (in proportion to its potential and mission) although it may be experiencing numerical additions from persons who have been a product of another church's growth, by the transfer of their membership.

What goes on within the fellowship of a church will indicate growth (or lack of it). A church which has become introverted may have its horizons raised and thus begin the process of growing. If it is a changing community where persons "unlike" itself moves in and the church endeavors to encompass the new group, it is growing, even though it may not as yet have contrived *how* it will reach them.

Time and place are to be considered. The seed sown may not take place until another *time* and another *place*. Some *plant* and others *water* and others *reap*. When a church begins to minister, in the name of Christ, to human needs, the product may not be accomplished as a citizen of the Kingdom for many years. But church growth is begun, even though those critics of ministry to church growth may condemn the ministry as "mere humanism" or "social work," while they themselves bask in the glorious harvest which they have gained by "preaching the Word." The church and its pastor who have given much time to sowing the seed is never quite so popular it seems as the person who has reaped the harvest. But here, again, is involved the problem of when to start counting.

Why not count anywhere and everywhere? Every man to the best of his ability of measurement. Taking into account community, church, and time and place, count the seeds sown, the buckets of water carried, and the bushels gathered. The height of the Christian can be measured in terms of his life, witness, stewardship, and love. It has been said that "by their fruits ye shall know them," and there must be some measurements for fruit. Like in a drought there won't be so many, or after abundant rains, many, or after a plague of *grasshoppers,* or after the discovery of an effective pesticide, et cetera.

To some, *church growth* brings up images of spurious mass evangelistic efforts which speak of nothing more than an emotional expression. They caution that such numbers added will give no great significance to the church. Often they are right. But wrong, if they conclude that all forms of mass evangelism are invalid and responses insincere. It was not so with Pentecost.

Others, so overtaken with abhorrence for a *"are you saved, brother,"* approach to lay or pastoral witnessing may have a tendency to reject the worth of direct personal witnessing at all. These will place their strength behind what they might call *cultivative witness.* This is sound logic. The greatest personal witness is given by a person who is obviously changed by his relationship to Christ and who in love and patience, can communicate this to another without having to say much about it. Too often though, the relationship established stops with being cultivative and loses its objective of witness.

Church growth to some is only what the church does as a whole in some far place, or in its competition with other faiths of the world. And they are partly right. A part of church growth is what the church does far away. But it will not do much far away if it is not growing locally.

In revulsion toward many churchmen who piously proclaim that they only *preach* the gospel, and imply that this has no relationship to practiced indignities to humanity, to hunger, justice, prejudice and war, there are those who say that Christ is best not proclaimed at all. That is, except as practiced in his concern for the hungry and maligned. Herein is involved the *great controversy* regarding the church and the world.

The church has always had problems with her relationship to the world, as pointed out by Paul L. Stagg in his book, *The Converted Church.*

In some instances, churches, seeking to remain uncorrupted by secular society, have withdrawn from the culture. These churches viewed their obligation as that of removing themselves from the profane world of business, politics, liberal education, public entertainment, and war, in order to establish a separate community of the elect. Consequently the church is looked upon primarily as the defender of orthodox beliefs and traditional morality. She becomes essentially a fortress into which Christians retreat and in which they seek to find their security against the onslaught of a corrupt society.

In other instances, churches, remembering only that they must be in the world, have become folk churches; as such, they identify with a particular culture and seek to preserve that. Too few churches have seen themselves as a mission of God in the world.

George W. Webber has described the true church as being an outpost of the kingdom of God, which has been placed in a particular spot in the world to bear witness to the lordship of Jesus Christ; a mission living by the foolishness of God in a world that sometimes hates it, or is indifferent and seeks to take it captive.

Webber further points out that any church that does not recognize the basic purpose for its existence may die, and that the church in America often does not recognize that it is in a missionary situation. Missions may be viewed only as a special project of the church, through which men and women are sent to preach in distant lands, overseas, in Indian territory, or in the inner city. We have forgotten that missions is the task of the church wherever it finds itself.

Dietrich Bonhoeffer observed that the church had relegated Christ to a relatively insignificant sphere of life where he had become a matter of only incidental interest. He believed that God should be at the center of life, not relegated to dwelling on the borders, not in weakness but in strength; not in man's suffering and death, but in his life and propriety; and that God is the "beyond" in the midst of our life. The church exists not where human powers give out, on the borders, but in the center of the village (*Letters and Papers from Prison*).

There is church growth potential where the "local" church is as long as there are people there.

Because the church is both in the world and not of it, her being feels the excitement of dwelling at the edge of a storm. She is a refuge for her people where they may find strength but also a battlefield where war is waged for the souls of men. Without this concept the church cannot minister and may not have validity as a church.

In recent years there has been a tendency toward a polarization to what has been called the "evangelistic" approach or "social action" approach to church growth. Groups have aligned themselves with one approach or the other and have vehemently shouted their derisions at the other camp. Only now does it appear that the forces toward polarization of position are diminishing, and it is apparent that neither "evangelism" nor "social action" is complete without the other, as has been discussed in *New Life in the Church,* by Robert A. Raines.

Extremists in either area are without sound theological sustenance. Evangelism which counts the soul saved who raised his hand and said, "I trust Jesus," and from that moment onward lived devoid of him, was never valid. Social action which regards only the worth of man is mere humanism and as such may be one of the worst forms of atheism.

True evangelism sees the plight of man in his spiritual emptiness and in his earthy locale. It speaks to him in a voice of compassion about his needs and helps him to discover that his greatest need is Christ.

This is precisely what Jesus did in his ministry. He *used* the environment and the human need to direct attention to the spiritual blessing that he could provide (the woman at the well, the adulterous woman, Bartimaeus). Professional Christian social workers sometimes are heard to apolgize for any apparent use of human need to direct the individual to Christ. They "love them for their human worth" apart from a concern to lead them to Christ. Such a stance on the surface may seem quite humble, loving, and Christian, but it intimates that the love which the worker has to give is as valuable and as redemptive as that which Christ has to give. We are messengers of Christ in reconciliation, not the creator.

In the secular world an individual does not object to being *used* by his employer to fill a worthwhile position and to receive lucrative benefits. Neither would he feel *used* by any friend who would direct him to such a position.

In areas of *rapidly growing population, as cities or suburban areas, church growth* may be simply accepted as the gathering of Christians who are unaffiliated with a local church. This produces local church growth but it cannot stop there. Members received are really the product of other churches' growth and the recipient of this growth, in return, must contribute to the church as a whole. She is often reluctant to do this. Anesthetized by the vast numbers she has gained, she is prone to think herself a success in terms of growth. She builds larger buildings, programs, and organizations, but hesitates to share her resources with those churches (viz. inner city or rural churches), which have made her what she is.

The First Baptist Church of Bellevue, Nebraska, is an interesting (and perhaps extreme) study in *receiving* and *giving*. Located in a small town adjacent to a large military establishment (Offutt Air Force Base), she made her beginning a little over a decade ago, largely as a church for Baptists who were stationed there. Her growth was phenomenal, in spite of the fact that the constituents were highly mobile. Rarely did any remain longer than three years. When this church was five years old she had received over one thousand members and only six families had been present when the church was originally organized. Her membership was about three hundred.

Frantically she worked to provide space, leadership, and programs for the highly mobile congregation, at the same time desperately desiring to be "church" to the needs of the surrounding community and the world. She wanted to give, as well as receive. Bearing in mind that her members would likely soon be members of other churches, she sought to endow them with a sense of mission and service which would be carried away with them. They would need training in Bible study, mission action, witness, stewardship, and practical service. As a training field the church established outposts in unchurched communities, a benevolent and witnessing center in the inner city of adjacent Omaha, music and recreation programs, educational programs, evangelistic and prayer groups, youth work, two coffeehouses, and numerous other expressions of the church to provide *some place* for growth for everyone.

In order for the church to maintain numerical growth she would have to receive over two hundred additions per year by transfer of membership and one hundred new converts. Today the church has over one thousand members (with an additional eight hundred in the new churches she established). She has "former members" in places like Turkey, Spain, Guam, Vietnam, Springfield, Massachusetts, and Puerto Rico, who are benefiting the churches there by what they learned as Christians in Bellevue, Nebraska. She has contributed pastors and other church vocational persons from her congregation.

The church is concerned about being indigenous. It *is* indigenous to the military personnel, but it wants more than this. It wants to reach local and civilian people. This it is accomplishing through its programs of outreach in the inner city, the coffeehouses, and its chapels in other communities.

There is a group of Christians which does not find church growth desirable at all. Although this group would not likely express itself in such an extreme way, it does personify a vast and malignant death-wish and evidence a rationale for despair. Only a few would venture an utterance of "God is dead."

These are largely those who for practical reasons have made their decisions. They have viewed their resources and concluded that the chasm is too deep, too wide to bridge in the effort to be instruments of God for his use in enlarging Christ's church. Frustration is the mark of our day. The decision to die, rather than to grow often finds its beginning thesis in something which is Christian in character but which does not give adequate consideration to the totality of the Christian faith.

The deep and valid hope of some to diminish the apparent fragmentation of the Christian faith may serve to diminish the faith itself. A sincere effort to consolidate the *organizations* of Christianity may overshadow the true *being* of the church. Thus, the goal to *regulate* obscures the objective to *propagate*. It is often noted that one church (local) which has divided into two churches will *each* produce as great growth as the original. Two consolidated will likely produce no more than one of the original ones. Admittedly, a simple statistic does not represent all the implications here. There are implications of competition, malice, envy, and injustice, but, also, there are implications toward a greater personalization in Christian service, more intimate location to people, and therefore, a wider opportunity to share the faith. These are not all the implications but the situations should be viewed from the standpoint of *ultimate* good for the total church's purpose, rather than that which is a part of the purpose. In this regard, however, it must be said that a lessening of the schisms of Christianity are important to church growth.

A decision to death may be made because of location of the church house itself (for many houses of churches do not permit the church to adequately function), an introverted theology of the church, or because the people have changed in the church community.

Many churches have found themselves strangled by their locations. It may have been that the church made a poor choice in locating itself in the beginning. Or highways, railroads, and encroaching businesses strangled its growth.

Church houses in themselves are great assets, or liabilities. In some areas their ornate beauty attracts seekers; in other areas they repulse. Some houses have been designed for a type of program or a form of gathering which is no longer relevant. Some houses have become a fetish which has claimed its devotees and exploited them of their reason for being "church."

Churches sometimes die because they too long have served themselves. They have developed an introverted theology. Their objective becomes that of creating the softest pews, the most satisfying music, the most exclusive *in* group. They would direct their programs toward reaching *our members* or *our children.* Their pastor will speak often of building a *quality* church, rather than a *quantity* church and will succeed in building neither.

Most threatening to the American church is the change of people in the church community. This is a phenomenon in nearly every community setting. Rural people move to town, urban people move to the country, inner city people move to the suburbs, ethnic groups move to the inner city. Expensive high-rise apartments locate in blue-collar areas, low-rent housing replaces old factories and the church is in a dilemma. Once a church has established its "in" group, it is difficult to change. Even though the church itself may desire to change and struggle with its physiological identity, the community knows its historic identity, and is reluctant to accept another identity for the church. Too often though, the church does not or cannot change. It would rather "die than switch." Or, it might move. Like the rather prestigious "first" church which saw its surrounding community becoming made up of low-income people, bought a large acreage on the outskirts of town and after erecting a magnificent building placed a sign in front with the words, "We Care."

It is not easy for a church to minister to a changing community. Yet, how it seems to adversely reflect upon the church when it fails to do so!

A church in a suburban area of a large city has seen over ten years of good growth. She erected beautiful buildings and found an acceptable role in missions around the world. Her membership was made up of families of successful, white businessmen. They were progressive; the church program was rather complete. A Negro dentist bought an expensive home in the community. Then Negro businessmen, teachers, and other professionals bought homes.

The church was challenged.

The emotional and spiritual struggle which followed would appear abhorrent to Christians in other places. Yet, if these looked close at hand they might note a "for sale" sign on their own church house because "others" had moved into the church community.

At first it seemed that the church might prove her faith. It would stay!

In response to the question as to whether or not the church would continue with its building program and expect to grow, a layman said, *"If it should be that we desire to protect our church from the changing community, we should buy acreage outside of town, build a fence around it, and we, with our church house, move inside. On the other hand, if we wish to be a church, then here, on this corner, in the midst of change is where we best should be."* The congregation built a new auditorium.

But polarization and indecision began. Some members of the congregation moved away, a vociferous minority became exclusive in their attitudes regarding the membership of the church and established a "protectorate." Their viewpoint was, *"We can't afford to permit the blacks to come; more people will leave and we can't keep up the payments on the church building." "Better to lose the house than the church,"* others replied.

The practical constituency prevailed. The racial schism became greater. The summer Bible school which had been an agency of enlistment was announced quietly to the members. The basketball goals on the outdoor court were removed because blacks were playing there after school. The new gymnasium was closed. Lay visitation in the community was discontinued.

Members who had contributed financially when the church seemed ready to witness to the whole community were repulsed at the object of their giving. The dilemma, coupled with the morbidity of a dying church, would bring them to despair and ultimately the moral necessity to leave the church.

The remaining membership were no less distraught. Although their racial apologetic would not create the moral necessity to leave the church, they did not enjoy the crises provoked for those who did leave. They had loved them in those days when it was easier for the church to be a church. And they were troubled about the Christian "rightness" of their own view. Later, in other churches many would take an opposite view and urge that their church minister to any newcomers.

And so, like pallbearers taking the earthy remains of a loved one from whom the spirit has departed to his burial, they moved to sell the building and dispose of the estate. A final bequest being made to missions—in Africa.

Less dramatic than this have been the choices of churches to die. The causes are not always so explicitly drawn, nor the "sides" so momentarily popular. The dividing line is far more likely to be class than color in the typical American church. More insidious is death that comes to churches where no sides are ever drawn and there are no divisive issues. In such a church, death comes on like terminal cancer—slowly, slowly—then life is gone.

2 Why Grow?

Because:
of God's redemptive plan
God seeks
. . . and draws to himself
. . . and works through men
. . . and through his Son
. . . and through his church
. . which does not always have the right concept of what a church is and should do
as:
. . . some do not wish to grow—"let God do it."
. . . imperialism
. . . religion relativism
. . . mere proclamation of having "found"
. . . restriction to a pulpit performance
. . . exclusivism
. . . institutionalization
And God finds
. . . in partnership with a church which is
. . an outpost of God
. . a fellowship with eternal implications
. . a testimony of God acts
. . a harbinger of hope
. . a constituency of spiritual possibility
. . a dynamic of the Holy Spirit
. . an organism of action
Such a church practices what it knows
. . . and the pastor is the key
. . . and there are mission action groups
. . . and implementation by communication of the message
which is discussed
in the next chapter.

Churches which grow will have within themselves a motivation to growth. This cannot be taken for granted. They will not grow unless they are motivated to do so. An intentional effort must be made to accomplish motivation. It will incorporate a knowledge of God's redemptive plan for all mankind, an understanding of what the church is, and means for putting these concepts into action.

The pastor of a semi-rural Baptist church, the Pine Grove Baptist Church, Pineville, Louisiana, reported after his church nearly doubled its membership in two years, *"The greatest single step was for our church to decide that they had a job to do and say, 'We must begin to grow and do something for the Lord.' This was a beginning and from there young Christians mostly have continued to thrill our church and community."*

There are few thoughts of the Bible more impressive than that of God's great search for his creation; the search began with man's lostness and his right of choice between good and evil. Or, perhaps it was a choice between chaos and order, or, Paul Tournier might call it a place *"to be,"* from the *"no place of wandering"* (*A Place for You*).

The setting was one of peace and fulfilment. God's creation was ordered, with each component determining its part, each element had a purpose to fulfil and related itself to the product of the other elements that were there. These found completion within themselves. Then God placed man within it and gave him dominion over it, and God was there. Man could have existed within this idyllic beauty throughout eternity but God loved him and wanted him to be even more like himself. So, God put man in the role of yokefellow to work with himself in those creative acts of bringing order out of chaos.

There is the hypothesis that a chick new-hatched may form a leader image with the first object it perceives. Man newly created first saw his creator, but would God's Adam break from his embryo of paradise and follow God into the bright new world? Not always. Adam's kind would search for its "freedoms" and take long to discern that freedom does not find its answer in freedom itself, but only in the place "to be."

God watched. Paradise dissipated itself with man's foolish rationale that God cannot find him, even in his lostness. Newfound freedom goads man to find a hiding place. Yet, in bushes and man-made coverings, man cannot hide the piercing question, *"Where art thou?"* The question speaks of loneliness. God's. It intimates his great concern that the creative act which he began is not yet complete. Man still has longed for chaos, though order has been exemplified in his creation. God wants him back to complete that perfection which he began and he longs for the restoration of those glorious times when the two of them, God and man, could talk together in the cool of the garden's day.

The search begins, and presses ever onward to find the individual, to speak to him from the burning bush and serpent upon a pole, and ram caught by horns in the thicket, and Son upon a tree.

Isaiah joined the great God-search as he heard his "Whom shall I send?" and responded with a "Here am I, send me." Christ cemented God's yokefellow concept of search with his: "As the Father has sent me, even so send I you." The early church joined the search party of God for the lost of his creation. They went to Rome, Corinth, Philippi and Antioch, Egypt, and possibly to Spain. They sought for the lost on the highways and in the hedges and on the road to Ethiopia, and in the streets and beside the rivers. The years wore on and the theology of search became sometimes lost in vaulted cathedrals and in "positions" in the name of Christ and in searchings for the Holy Grail. Though born with the God-garden image, man was unwilling yet to respond with "here am I." The lost world set about to fabricate its own garden, and with its own hands to make a place to be which was peace and beauty and completion, but without God. Man formed his governments and laws. He proclaimed with each new creation of his hand that this was paradise, but knew that it was not. Each succeeding generation contrived its own devices to prevent the inevitable briar patch which grows on things solely made by the hands of man. The church, too, opted out of this joint search-plan with God. It developed its own theology, a rationale, which said in essence, "If God wants them let him find them." The church had found other enjoyable things to do. It could become a pawn of courts and was able to smile benignly at the heartaches of man who wandered in his wilderness. It could claim its "rightful" place in the orderless society and adapt itself to its environment of prestige and affluence. God's "Whom shall I send?" found no response from church houses, or chaplains of the court. In fact, the question was not even heard.

Although the ears of God's yokefellows were stopped with the wax of a deafening rationale, God still could scream to them from a secular world. In the latter part of the eighteenth century, Captain James Cook set out on his explorations of the world. In his journals recounting his explorations, he commented on the destitute plight of people of many nations, especially those of the Sandwich Islands of the Pacific. Even one who had not been "sent" on God's great search could discern that a place without his principles of order was a frightfully disordered place.

A Baptist shoe cobbler in England, William Carey, read the *Journal* and heard God's plea for help. His response of "Send me" was not met with enthusiasm on the part of the church. Finally, however, he was able to enunciate the theology of search in such a way as to encourage some to send him in their behalf. The attempt to go to the Sandwich Islands, however, was defeated. God wanted him in India and Burma. His going would launch new enthusiasm on the part of many Christians to join in God's search for the lost of the world. The church's newfound mission, though, would soon be exploited by the mercenaries who saw that Christianity might abet their efforts to establish new economies. Governments which had historically found a close affinity with the establishment of a church would also exploit the search purpose for the causes of colonizing new worlds.

In this cross-purpose of what the world would have it be and what God would have it be, the church often turned again to its old processes of developing a logic for whatever behavior it wished to enact. This process continues to the present time and perhaps it always will, depending upon the sophistication of the culture and the ability of Adam's kind to turn a theological truth to an enigma.

Many manifestations on the perversion of the theology of search are extant today. The overhang of yesterday's commercial and empirical reasonings are still being expressed. The confusion of thought that affluence is synonymous with Christianity is felt in many parts. Not only is this true in the case of American Christianity extended to less Christianized nations of the world, but it is true in America as well. Efforts of the comfortable middle-class church to "missionize" an underprivileged area of its locality may produce little more than empty souls garbed in better garments. And the church, having accomplished this, sees its task as ended before it has ever uttered the question, "Where art thou?" in behalf of God. This is not to minimize the importance of the church performing works in the name of Christ and being concerned with what the individual wears. It is, however, to negate a theology that God is only concerned with what the individual wears.

A church of ethnic or cultural groups may reproduce itself in another area, gathering only those who are similar groups and thus reflecting the age-old influences of imperialism.

That propagation of Christianity which utilizes cultural entities is significant to God's great plan of search, but to use the Christian faith as a mere tool to continue a culture is an invalid use of the Christian faith.

Another more recent perversion of the search theology relates to religious relativism. A wider understanding of the religious faiths of the world has brought some to conclude that one faith is as good as another. The proponents of this idea have come to their conclusions without the firm conviction that Christ is the Alpha and the Omega. The idea springs from a tenet of the Protestant Christian faith which acknowledges the priesthood of the believer and his right to determine his relationship with God. In this instance, the responsibility to influence for Christ is terminated when the choice has been made, even though that choice may be an error. The search in behalf of God stops there then, more in recognition of the state which mankind has elected for himself than in deference to the state God desires for man. It does not see other than Christian religions as being an imperfect man-concept of God, but sees them as being complete within themselves and as valid as the Christian faith.

Such religious relativism expresses itself in less extreme forms within the Christian faith. It would become permissive in this regard to believe anything about Christ, to approve any immorality, and to say it doesn't really matter what you believe. It becomes a kind of situation ethic.

The story is told of a little mountain church made up of a few individuals who were barely literate and who had come across the passage in the Scripture, *"without the shedding of blood there is no remission of sin."* The group considered this passage for some time, but the consideration was apart from the biblical context and significance of the passage. It was decided by consensus that it was the responsibility of the congregation to shed blood for the remission of sins. So, upon a certain night they set out in single file across the mountains, determined that when their course intersected that of some individual it would be taken to mean that God had intended that person die as the remission for the sins of the whole group. Ultimately, they came upon the house of an elderly woman and took her life. The position of the Christian relativist would reason "who has a right to draw the lines, what is Christian? What is not Christian?" The people simply were doing what they believed was right.

Certainly this is an extreme illustration, but the Christian relativist is hard put to propagate his faith.

A less extreme concept of Christian relativism is commonly exemplified contemporarily in the attitudes that since all Christian denominations have validity, every effort must be made to keep them from being competitive with each other. Competition in this instance is interpreted as being something unbecoming and unchristian. It does not acknowledge that in the secular world an enjoyable community can be made up of more than one grocery store, or more than one drugstore, or more than one doctor, all of which appeal to the different likes and dislikes of the community. Presence of more than one such entity could well contribute to a climate of creativity and investigation of the best avenues of communication and the higher quality of products and service.

We have seen this logic displayed in America to the extent that if a church, as a congregation, should die in a community its last will and testament may be that the property of the church may not be used for any Christian purpose. The reason that is given may be that it is not desirable to evidence to the world that one church may be better able to witness than another. This would indicate a preeminence of one over another. Although there is scriptural verity to the concept, it subjects the greater witnessing imperative of the church to a lesser dogma. (For example: It is *most* important that the church not display to the world any evidence of fragmentation.)

Much of the religious relativism concept, or in this instance Christian relativism, is reflected in extreme efforts toward organizational ecumenicity today. In many ways, this is an age of ecumenicity, rather than an age of Christian mission. It is recognized, of course, that true ecumenicity is an imperative of the church. The church is the body of Christ and in this body we, as Christians, find unity. Temporal and organizational expressions of this are not as important as what the church is by nature. If the desire to organizational ecumenicity overrides the imperative of the church to witness, or to join with God in his divine search for the lost, then human organization which is called the church may not even be the church. In this regard, it must be understood, however, that ecumenical organization has great validity if their purpose is to abet the plan of bringing man to God through Jesus Christ.

The *search* theology has found a confusion in the thought of some that one need only to proclaim the lost to be found and the fact is accomplished. The state-church concept reflects this idea somewhat. For example, a person who was born within the jurisdiction of a state became a member of that state's church. Or, as in an earlier day of mission effort in the Far East, it is reported that a missionary gathered about him a crowd of people and suddenly threw a bucket of water on the assemblage and thereby proclaimed them baptized in the name of Christ. These two are also extreme illustrations, but they find their pragmatic demonstration in the body of many churches which "pronounce" some to be "found."

Additionally, search may become restricted to a confined performance from behind the pulpit. Here the church, perhaps through its pastor, shouts its message to a world beyond the church house walls, but the world outside can't hear because of the walls.

God's searching is often inhibited by churches which are selective in the areas of their search in his behalf. Some churches may limit their search to only those who are like themselves. That is, they have the same kind of houses, or wear the same kind of clothes, or have approximately the same incomes, or they speak the same language, or they are from the same country, or have the same color of skin.

Whenever the church becomes exclusive in its searching it has captured what it has called the church from God and called their will his.

Most common of the search heresies may be the institutionalization of the search. That is, at some point, the Christian body discovers a means whereby the search is effectively consummated. The means which has produced abundantly is then institutionalized and charged with the responsibility for propagating the search. This might take the form of a hospital, or a school. It could be a Sunday School, or a church choir. It might be a morning worship service. The institution thus established is remembered and revered. It was a good thing. It accomplished a good purpose.

As the years went by the Christian participant became less an individual participant in God's search, but was willing to endow the good means of the institution so that it might continue with the search. The establishment, then, thus endowed with good intentions of an earlier year begins to find itself isolated from the purpose of search. It is in a secular world, and secular agencies have established institutions that are very similar in purpose, such as hospitals for ministering to the sick and educational institutions for the purpose of teaching. And so, in order to protect its integrity as an institution operating in the midst of surrounding secular groups, it begins to identify itself more and more with these and to announce that its curriculum, or service, or community, is just as good as the secular ones and becomes competitive on a secular basis. The endower of this institutionalized enterprise may have forgotten to notice that the institution to which he committed his part in God's plan for search is no longer searching. Perhaps if he has noticed, he does not care as much as once he did, and now he hides in the small brush of his garden and responds to God's, "Where am I?" by saying, "The institution which I established in your name is there before you, ask of it."

If the theology of search were adequately comprehended and practiced, would this be all of it? Does God ask no more of us than that we seek? Have we any responsibility to find?

Many times one may have witnessed in various ways to find that there was no response to his seeking. Some good friend, noticing the discouragement, has come to say, "You've done the best you can; you are only responsible to sow the seed." Can this be accepted conscientiously? The comfort that the words could bring would be helpful but it is hard to find personal satisfaction from seed that are sown which bring no harvest. Does God send us into fields that are white unto harvest simply to see they are white and do need harvesting and that the workers are few? Can it be conceived that he would send a shepherd to seek a lonely lost sheep and discover that he is frightened and the sheep is enmeshed in briers, his skin is torn, and the shepherd can only pronounce, "You are lost"? So much Scripture is involved with the Christian's responsibility in finding too.

Christian workers often have labored hard and long in fields that have not produced. They have not found. Sacrificially they went to search. Gave up careers or marriage, success in a secular world, in order to seek, but never found. These have engendered great sympathy and indeed they should, for have not they staked all to seek, and were not rewarded with the find? It is true there are some fields where some are intended to sow and others reap, and the consequence of time will indicate the kind of seed, the kind of ground, the kind of harvest. God makes the final measure of the worker. Certainly it is Christ who builds his church and we are his witnesses. We need to be careful, however, that by small, or little, response we are not tempted by our martyr complex to remember how sacrificially we spent and how poor was our reward.

What Is the Church?

An adequate theology of the church is at the heart of any strategy for church growth. It is basically understood that the church is:

1. AN OUTPOST OF GOD.—The church is a part of the purpose of God. Found in the heart of God, it is of his plan. It is born of him, part of the body of Christ, locally or in a larger sense. The church is much of what lost men see and hear of Christ. The church is what we as churchmen, as Christians, do

about Christ in the place where we live. As God's mission into the world the church is to be in it, but not of it.

The Christian is a citizen of the kingdom of God and yet of the earth. He stands with one foot in the mud and one in the Promised Land, contending with his frustrations, his tensions, his trials, yet made stronger because of the conflict within himself. He is a man and yet a child of God. It is a marvelous conflict.

2. A FELLOWSHIP WITH ETERNAL IMPLICATIONS.—This fellowship is a "holding all things in common," which was identifiable with that early church. This sharing of what each had, and was, is significant to the methodology of church growth. In that day, Christians held all things in common. Their community extended beyond the social relationships of man to fellowman; it extended into vertical relationship to Christ. And in the moment that relationship participated in what he is, it became eternal in its implications. It extended beyond that moment and beyond this moment, and the fellowship of church became past, present, and future. It was Alpha and Omega. The fellowship which *we* know in Jesus Christ extends to the life of every Christian who has lived—to everyone who will live.

3. THE TESTIMONY OF GOD-ACTS, AND ESPECIALLY OF HIS REDEMPTIVE PLAN.—Christians amount to little unless they are testifying to what God has done. In the early church, they often stood to say, "*This is what God has done.*" The sermon of Peter at Pentecost began with this God-act. In his sermon Stephen told about the God-act. The blind man who was healed, when asked what had happened said, "*I just couldn't tell you. I only know that whereas I was blind, now I can see.*" The church is a testimony to the God-acts—to what God has done, especially in his redemptive plan.

4. A HARBINGER OF HOPE.—The church is a hopeful institution, a hopeful involvement in the world. It is an exclamation of God's hope for mankind. Here we can fasten our wagon to a star. We need not die. We need not fail, for the church exemplifies hope—God's hope for mankind. It is a balm

of Gilead to the world's hurt. It is the salve that covers up the burning and the stinging, the odious hurt of the world.

5. A CONSTITUENCY OF SPIRITUAL POSSIBILITY, GARBED IN FLESHLY BODIES.—The church is frightfully visible, and is being criticized today because it can be seen. People know what the church is and what we are as parts of the church.

6. A DYNAMIC OF THE HOLY SPIRIT.—No earthly entity is like the church with such power, visibility, and assurance of success. But no church can truly grow without the endowment of the Holy Spirit.

7. AN ORGANISM OF ACTION.—There is a reciprocal action of God to the church and through it and the action of its earthy-clad constituency to God and to fellowman, because of Christ.

The members of this Christ-body who are the church cannot linger long as recipients of his Presence without bearing witness to that Presence to those who do not know him. Herein is reflected the great dual, yet inseparable commandment, "*to love God completely and to love one's fellowman as self.*" It is of major concern that churches be true to the New Testament form and continue to propagate similar organisms. The establishment of such churches finds importance in bringing men to God through Jesus Christ.

Church growth may not always be determined by the number of church units organized. Two churches of very small membership and weak leadership will probably be little more effective than a larger one. On the other hand, dynamic church growth is not produced by very large churches who have committed most of their Christian witness to the staff members whom they employ.

New churches often find an easy beginning when established upon the common ground that persons have for their place of cultural origin or human likes. Although this may be a real asset in the beginning, it poses a later problem to the church in breaking from her cultural isolation and in having redemptive meaning in a world of great cultural diversity. The church, in order to grow, must actively engage in breaking down barriers, rather than creating them. This does not, however, disparage the use of cultural or sociological entities.

A knowledge about God's redemptive plan and the work of the church is not enough. Church members must be motivated to an actual practice of what they know is right. But how to do this?

The pastor is the key. Although much must be said about the responsibilities of laymen, it is to be noted that there is little growth of any kind taking place in churches in which the pastor has not played the key role. He should *equip* the saints, but it is not likely they will be *well equipped* unless he shows them how. In nearly every instance of exciting church growth, the pastor is the major motivator. He informs of why and he shows them where or how. After this is accomplished then there are many ways in which the motivation is continued by laymen.

Pastor Charles A. Nowlen, Sr., of the United Methodist Church, Parker, Colorado, has worked with congregational development in ten states and in many different projects. Some of these have had an annual growth of over one hundred members, while some have started more slowly and developed gradually with great spiritual power. He involved his members in a house-to-house survey of the community and then followed this by leading the laymen in evangelistic visitation. He utilized neighborhood house meetings, thus "surrounding each person with the love of the church."

The pastor of the Goodyear Baptist Church, Picayune, Mississippi, Arlis F. Grice, through preaching and leading his laymen to personal witnessing, has led his church to add 499 members (151 of these new converts) in six years. The members of the church are involved in prayer and personal visitation to newcomers and persons in crisis.

The Tower Grove Baptist Church of St. Louis, Missouri, of

which E. Warren Rust is pastor, lost in total membership in a five-year period, but *added* 1,302 new members in the same period of time. The loss in membership was due to a transient mid-city location and the intrusion of two new interstate highways. The church involves its membership in church growth through a program called LIFE (Love Is for Everyone). Its members work daily in outreach and witness in four areas around the church building. *"Prayer is basic,"* the pastor reported. The church has a day-care ministry, summer camp program, day camp in the summer, golden age groups, marriage counseling clinics, family life conferences, referral contacts with community services, rehabilitation groups; has sponsored five mission chapels and experienced six hundred fifty professions of faith in ten special evangelistic services in this time. For motivational involvement, the growing churches use mission action groups of women and men missionary organizations, missions committees, reports from specialized workers and missionaries, and many other appropriate means.

Pastor M. Laurel Gray of the Church of the Covenant (Lutheran) of Gardena, California, reports that their whole program *"is designed to train the layman for his mission in the community."* This is a one-year-old church which added fifty-six in its glorious year. It meets in rented facilities.

In all these instances of growth (although the pastor has been unwilling to note his own importance), the growth has taken place because of the pastor's concept of God, the church, his calling, and his ability through the power of the Holy Spirit to motivate his church.

3 Communication Is Witness and Involvement

Church growth is dependent upon communication
. . which begins with one
. . is enlarged to two
. . and becomes a corporate witness
Some aspects of communication are
. . that it is a hopeless task
. . but the world is waiting
. . hopefully
Why communicate?
Because
. . we have answers
. . and we need the personal fulfilment
. . then too,
God said to
How communicate?
. . with love
. . and personal experience
. . through preaching and the worship service
. . and organization and programs
. . music and drama
. . recreational programs
. . CRISES
. . specific groups
. . and small groups
. . ministering
. . cultural and language groups

An adequate church growth is dependent upon an adequate communication of those things that are essential to church growth. This is witness and involvement. The communication of the person of Jesus, for example, must begin with a person who knows Jesus and can communicate something of what he is by what they are. This is but the beginning of that communication, however, since one person cannot possibly communicate all that Jesus is by relating the experience of what he is in meaning to himself. Having established the first bridge of communication, the communicator may be able to help the communicant enlarge his field of knowledge of Jesus by pointing him to additional resources such as: another person of greater spiritual knowledge, the biblical revelation, the historical revelation, the speaking of the Holy Spirit, and of prayer.

A third stage of this communication (witness) experience may become the developed community wherein the original communicator and the communicant join together in a mutual affirmation of the experience of the person of Jesus and collectively may begin the process of communication in behalf of Jesus all over again. This latter stage of communication is what the church does to effect church growth.

It must be remembered that church growth is not primarily concerned with those statistics which say that "the Grace Church or the Calvary Church has more members than it had a year ago," but it is concerned about the quantitative enlargement of the church in terms of its being a part of a wider acceptance of the personhood of Christ. This will most likely reflect itself in visible and numerical enlargement, but that in itself is largely a by-product of the major purpose of communicating Christ.

This treatment of communication (witness) and church growth is to deal with a few aspects of communicating the Christian faith. There are many forms of communication which can be considered within the scope of Christian communication, such as prayer and communication with other Christians. These are very important and a knowledge of these is essential to an adequate communication of the faith. The concern here, however, is with some basic considerations of how the church can grow by communicating itself to those who do not know Christ.

Eugene A. Nida, in his book *Religions Across Cultures,* has said that, to many persons the communication of the Christian faith is a hopeless task. In the first place, Christianity is considered to be no longer relevant in a technological society and a "post-Christian" era. For some radical theologians, not only is the belief in God dead, but God himself is nonexistent, and therefore belief in him is not only false but irrelevant.

Secondly, the church has not always responded well to the challenges of the day. Despite courageous efforts on the part of some few individuals, the church as a whole has not distinguished itself in facing up to controversial issues.

Peter L. Berger's *The Noise of Solemn Assemblies* describes religion in America as a starry-eyed optimism and a naive credulity in the ideology of the status quo; also, religion is something that goes well together with an unthinking, if benign conservatism in all areas of life.

Nida continues, that the average layman is frustrated because many theologians and church leaders are most pessimistic about the future of the church and the relevance of Christian faith. For many people, God may as well abdicate and let his ministers go into exile in the secular world.

Yet, despite the pessimism of church leaders and the often ineffectiveness of the church as an organized institution, the modern world is experiencing a biblical renewal of unprecedented proportions. The demand for Scriptures has grown greatly within the last few years, so that the United Bible Societies almost tripled their circulation in the years 1964-67, reaching a total of about 100 million copies of Bibles, New Testaments, Gospels, and selections.

Despite the claim that the Bible is no longer intelligible to modern man, there are more people reading and studying the Scriptures, whether individually or in small groups, than at any time in the history of Christianity.

In spite of the fact that there have been so many pessimisms expressed regarding church growth, and the fact that many mainline denominations are seemingly exercising "the death wish" to get away from it all, it seems that this day affords the greatest opportunity for communicating the gospel of Christ the world has ever known.

If there were a choice of any time in the period of history wherein to perform the most significant ministry for the cause of Christ's kingdom, it should be *this day*. *This day* offers opportunities because of the fact that the established church has been questioned and is now questioning itself—seeking to find new avenues of communicating the gospel on that basis which it can communicate. *This day*, because the "secular society" has moved in, and the Christian is not so much seeking to find out how to live in God's world for a while and in the "world's" world for a while, but how to live as Christians in God's world. *This day,* because of the advanced technological means of communication and transportation; because of the advances in concepts of psychology, medicine, labor, and community. There are no perfect answers to problems, but there is a better knowledge of how to deal with problems than in any previous day, and it can better be accepted that the advent of problems is an open door to a creative solution.

In order to communicate the gospel and make the church grow, it is assumed that one knows who he is and who Christ is and has a faith which is worthy of propagation.

Why Communicate?

It is necessary for the Christian to communicate, or witness, because he is a citizen of the Kingdom and a citizen of the world. As citizens of the Kingdom he has "good news" for the world. If he were only a citizen of the world he would recognize there were deadly problems on every hand and because these problems affected his environment and happiness he would wish to find solutions for them. He would come to have humanistic concerns because he would ultimately learn that the welfare of fellow humans had a direct relationship to his own welfare. Humans are busy in our world trying to do something about human needs. They are willing to make extreme sacrifices to see that human needs and problems are dealt with. Some even invest sums of money and have set up foundations to deal with human needs. There are movements to meet needs in the areas of government, economics, nutrition, health, welfare, education, pollution, population explosion, race, unemployment, civil rights, and others. But real answers are not found simply by humanistic concerns. Forced racial integration may lead to a greater racial antagonism. Compulsory education may lead to a decision simply not to learn. New clothes given to replace ragged ones become ragged in their turn and the problem is not permanently alleviated. Food given to those who desparately hunger is soon expended and hunger sets in again.

Human needs are important and God is concerned about them. Sometimes it may be that he has been able to point up these needs more directly to his "lost" world than through his "saints." The hippie movement may be an illustration of this point. The young people have abandoned the establishment and its possible concepts that the highest value of life comes from "things" by going barefooted and long-haired in the streets bearing tidings calling for love and peace. Through such a movement as this God may be pointing to an answer to the problem for them, to help them discover that they need love and peace. But they cannot find the answer to love and peace except through the citizens of his Kingdom.

At a meeting in New York in 1969, a group of church leaders were informed by interested civic leaders of crisis in the inner city of Harlem. Rioting and anarchy had led to a total abandonment of respect for property. Vast blocks of buildings, including stores and apartments, had been destroyed because the inhabitants of the area had become angry with absentee landlords; with inequities in their lives, as in their inability to find jobs, and to escape the dilemma of the ghetto. Because of this, the meeting was called to hear the plight of government, labor, and management in the community. There was a note of despair. *"What shall we do?"* was asked. Acceptable answers had been sought; better forms of management and of government, a willingness to accept a lesser share of profits, to settle for anything as long as there was order, were offered. Laws have not provided the answer. Conscientious humanitarian concerns had not provided the answer. The civic leader turned to the church leaders and asked, *"What is the answer, we believe you have it."*

The Christian must communicate the *"good news"* because he does have the answers. He does have the answer to war, peace, hate, rioting, vanity, violence, and violation of property rights of others. He does have the answer to injustice, and to life itself—life here and in the hereafter. Because he does have the answers, and is concerned about this world in which he lives, he cannot remain silent. He must become involved with the communication of the *"good news."*

Secondly, he must communicate, because it provides a personal fulfilment and expression of what he is in Christ. It must be done in order to effect a completion of his person in union with his person. Many Christians have experienced that joyous moment of fulfilment when he has seen what happens when he has been able to become involved in communicating the *"good news."*

A short while ago the Worcester Baptist Church, Worcester, Massachusetts, conducted an outdoor evangelistic crusade. A church choir from Dallas, Texas had just concluded the singing of a comtemporary folk musical which was performed on the parking lot. Pastor Bob Tremaine had spoken a few minutes regarding the *"good news"* which would be the hope of those who had gathered there. It was a rather strange assembly which was hearing that word. There were the elderly, well-dressed people. There were members of the church. There was a vast majority of people, however, who had simply come from the streets. There were several obviously "hippie" types.

Two men were sitting together in the congregation. One of them was paying intent attention to what Bob had to say. When an invitation for response was offered a strange expression came over his face. He nudged the man who was standing beside him and they pushed to an outer aisle. It appeared that they were about to leave, perhaps to have another drink of wine or simply walk out. But they stopped at the edge of the aisle. One of the men motioned to a young woman who was standing at the periphery of the crowd. She came and stood beside him and they talked earnestly. He talked as well to his friend. Then the three of them began to make their way toward the front. The transition of expression which took place in their faces was impressive. It was as though a light had begun to shine. There faded away the unkempt appearance, the dulness from their eyes. A new brightness seemed to emanate from them as they moved toward the front to make their profession of faith in Christ. Communication had been real. For those Christian workers who had been a part of making this setting for communication possible, it must have been a moment of fulfilment.

The communication evidenced here was but the ripened fruit of all that had taken place before through the efforts of an *involved* congregation. A small group of Christians (twenty-two), with the aid of the Southern Baptist Convention, had purchased a large, unused church building in the inner city of Worcester. They were *motivated* from the beginning with a desire to communicate through involvement. Their involvement was incredible for so small a group.

Their worship service was a kind of strategy meeting where their plans for involvement were involved with God. Each member saw himself in light of what talents he had and could use. They studied the community's needs and determined how they would relate redemptively to these. The needs were many. There were dope addicts, "winos," elderly people in a modern high-rise apartment across the street from the church house. There was a college, multiracial groups, acres of low-rent tenements, hundreds of children playing on the streets, business people, and older youth without purpose.

Like leaven, the church began to grow. The vast sanctuary of the church house, with its high-vaulted ceilings, would seat thirteen hundred people, but for a time would be the least-used portion of the building. The parking lot provided a skating rink for the children of the streets. A drug rehabilitation center was provided in the basement and interested persons "outside" the local congregation assisted with the work. An after-school program, a day-care program, and a mother's club were established.

In response to the many crisis needs, the church established a "crisis phone" so that those at the point of suicide, or in a drug coma, or with family problems, could find help. A hospital made beds available for emergency use. The city offered its service. The Junior Chamber of Commerce helped man the phones. The radio and television stations announced the "crisis phone" number. A large motel carried the number on its outdoor announcement sign.

Bible study groups were established in the homes of members; a youth forum was conducted at the college; Bible day camps were carried out throughout the city. Ball clubs were organized in the parks. Some members taught Puerto Rican immigrants to read English.

Then, there was *Lost and Found,* the coffeehouse operated in the church basement. Accouterments were not physically lavish, such as the electrical wire spool tables, early "tenement house" chairs, the stage for performances, and the lighting. The spiritual furnishings were from a contemporary *Book of Acts.* There was a copy of *Good News for Modern Man,* Today's English Version on every table.

Older members of the church moved from table to table to bear witness to every group. Newer members served the tables and often joined the groups to tell what Christ had done for them. Now and then, after a musical performance, a performer spoke of Christ, though the music might well have been "hard rock." On some nights as many as 150 people waited outside for their "turn" to come in and hear the good news.

Chapels, with worship services and educational programs, were conducted in surrounding communities by lay leaders who had become involved in the program of their church.

New members were nurtured by older members (perhaps only a few months older) and helped to find their place of creative witness.

The church reached over 1,000 people a week in the influence of its being. In such an event of "mass evangelism" as earlier described in the account of the parking lot meeting there were 115 professions of faith.

But, again, it must be noted that the "response" was but a beautiful culmination of personal involvement of the life of a church in the lives of people. It was the beginning of an experience for the New Christians in fulfilment by witness.

The Christian is always strengthened by his testimony of what Christ is to him; so is the church. Whenever a church has come to the point that it is no longer able to communicate this "good news" to a lost world, it is missing its great blessing of fulfilment. And this blessing of fulfilment is so important that, if missed, the church cannot live and grow.

The third reason that communication is necessary is that it is God's imperative. This "have to" commission to communicate is mentioned lastly because if the first two "whys" haven't been accomplished, then a "have to" commandment is resented. Perhaps too many church members are carrying out the command to go, simply because they feel that God has said they must. They enter into the miraculous venture, commissioning missionaries to go in their behalf to countries far away, or to people who are remote from their immediate community and feeling that this is all of it, but missing its blessing.

It is true that we know we are children of God if we keep his commandments. But keeping commandments must be a desire that stems from the heart and involves the whole being in meeting the needs of the world in the name of Christ, thereby learning the inner fulfilment which comes from the venture. The Christian, with gladness then, hears his command to go and is thrilled that he has spoken, delighted that he has offered the opportunity to speak in his behalf.

Consider now some ways in which communication is accomplished. Reuel L. Howe, in *The Miracle of Dialogue*, says in essence that every man is a potential adversary, even those we love, and that it is only through dialogue (or communication) that we are saved from this enmity toward one another. Communication is love and when this love stops, love dies and resentment and hates are born. But communication can restore this dead relationship. Indeed this is the miracle of dialogue (communication or involvement). Relationships are brought into being and those relationships which have died can be made to live again.

The *beginning* of communication truly *is love*. No one is ever able to speak to another adequately until he is convinced that he can love the other. This is the most important credential in communicating. It involves the ability to love, even though the person who is being loved does not deserve it at all, and may be most unlovely. That was the basis of Christ's communication. He loved us when we were most unlovable. In reciprocation, we must love the object of our communication even though he may be very unlovable.

A few years ago a young man was called to a church in the mountains of Kentucky. He had previously had a very pleasant ministry in another section of the country. He had been successful. The church to which he was called was a church of great potential. It was really a church of greatness. But the young pastor stayed only a short while, and on his leaving, said with a depth of sorrow to a friend, "I could not understand them enough to love them." His frankness was a little startling, but all of us have had that problem at one time or another. We can become antagonistic toward those people whom we do not understand simply because we would not hear them long enough to love them, and could not love them enough to communicate to them. There are those who are excellent missionaries to people who are down and out, but on the other hand cannot really appreciate the needs of those who are "up and out." They suffer the inability to love enough to communicate. Churches across our land have moved rapidly from the inner city with all of its turmoil and all of its hatreds to the suburbs. The suburbs must be where more lovable people live. It is hard to love the teen-ager who is angry and rebellious, exceptionally hard to love a militant or an anarchist. Indeed, it is hard to love an alcoholic who lies in the gutter. It is almost impossible to love a person who is dragged down with drug addiction and who threatens our own system of values.

Reuel L. Howe, in *Herein Is Love*, says in a discussion of the kind of love which is communication, that love is too commonly regarded as a sentiment and emotion which are certainly parts of love, but are not synonymous with love. More is meant than that when we say, "God is love," or "Love your neighbor."

Love is a moving, creating, healing power of life and unites life with life, person with person, and is not easily discouraged. The most dramatic symbol of love's courage and triumph is the resurrection and the cross. It stands for the truth that Christ has loved us.

"Herein is love, not that we have loved God, but that he loved" (1 John 4:10). We show our love for him by loving one another with his love. Our response to God's love is the work of the church. We show our love for God by loving one another and in this act we introduce one another to God. This is what the church does. It is the vocation of God's people.

If we participate in the love of God which is working in the world, we need to understand ourselves and our own human problems in relation to love. Christian love and its work should be a reckoning with the complications of human existence.

We communicate also through the relation of *personal experience*. As Paul said, "I know whom I have believed, and am persuaded that he is able to keep that which I have committed unto him against that day" (2 Tim. 1:12).

He was giving irrefutable evidence. It was irrefutable from the standpoint that no one could contradict Paul's testimony of what Christ meant to him. They might discredit Paul himself as to his intellectual evaluation or his spiritual experience, but for whatever Paul was worth, the testimony was worth that much. Peter's testimony at Pentecost was basically a testimony of what he knew God had done. Stephen's address at his stoning was a similar testimony of God's acting in his life. Every Christian has a personal testimony to give. To the man who knows him for whatever he is, the testimony is worth that much to the hearer.

We did not have the privilege (nor perhaps would have liked it) of making the journey to the moon as have our astronauts. We do not know what the moon surface is like, but the astronauts told us what it is like. We followed them in our imagination. We felt the soft touch of the surface of the moon. We imagined the texture of the moon dust and saw crystalline substances glimmering in the brilliant sun. Pictures were taken to document this experience. It could have all been a fraud, for we were not there, but we heard the personal testimony and it seemed real. The circumstances seemed to indicate that it all was true, and we believe a lot more about the moon than we did before the astronauts said they went there. So it is in the testimony of our Christian experience. If we believe that experience sufficiently and can communicate it, then there are many hearers who will believe.

Preaching and the worship program are means of communication or witness. It has been a very effective means for many in recent years. Great preachers have stood in pulpits and changed the lives of men by what they said about Christ and by what they spoke of from his Word. Jonathan Edwards brought a new vitality to the pulpit. George Whitefield stirred the hearts of many. Dwight L. Moody, Billy Sunday, Billy Graham, and all those of us who have ever preached have been able to communicate something to those who have heard.

The Cinco Baptist Church of Ft. Walton, Florida, grew from 157 members in 1957 to 1,287 members in 1969. The pastor reported, "Our church is built strictly upon the worship service and not from any organization. Our preaching services reach more people than any of the organizations. We have three services on Sunday and are planning a fourth." (Statement made by the pastor, Rev. Talmadge Smith, Cinco Baptist Church, Ft. Walton, Florida.)

Preaching is an important part of the life of any church. More and more in recent years, it has been heard most largely by those who already know Christ. It becomes increasingly difficult to get "the world" to come inside a house and hear the preacher preach. This does not mean that preaching has become any less important for it is a major means of communication. But the church does not dare to bear the responsibility of limiting its communication to only that which is said from the pulpit.

Communication and involvement are accomplished through *organization* and *program.* Church organizations and programs are very effectively used. From the turn of the twentieth century until about the mid-1950's, organizations and programs in churches were very effective instruments in communicating the gospel. This is not meant to say that organizations and programs are not important means of communication at the present time. Indeed they are. Any church which effectively communicates and brings about membership involvement must have organizations and programs. The organization of Sunday Schools, or such educational programs, has provided a unique teaching experience in which church growth is accomplished through small groups which are instructive, usually within the church house. Unenlisted persons, those who had not heard the good news, were brought inside and were enveloped with love and teaching that was exemplified within the class and by the Christian testimony of the teacher and Christian pupils in the group. Many of these were, and are, brought to a saving knowledge of Jesus Christ.

The First Baptist Church of St. Charles, Illinois, increased Sunday School attendance from 64 in 1967 to 132 in 1969, producing many new members for the church. The music and

Woman's Missionary organizations contributed to the spiritual growth, as well. (Report received from the pastor, C. Orville Kool.)

The First Church of God, Greenfield, Indiana, under the leadership of pastor Wayne E. Stout, increased in Sunday School attendance from 60 to 169 in a nine-year period. A major emphasis has been placed upon this educational organization which encourages personal witnessing and concern. (Report received from the pastor, Wayne E. Stout.)

Four hundred fifty people were baptized and 530 were added by transfer of membership to the Cameron Baptist Church, Lawton, Oklahoma, in a five-year period, ending in 1968. The pastor credits the church organizations, particularly Sunday School, Training Union, Woman's Missionary Union, and Brotherhood, for great assistance in this. Particularly insofar as they have "helped each individual Christian to witness each day to some person." (Report received from the pastor, Dan Pruitt.)

The Oak Grove Baptist Church of San Jose, California, is located in a fast-growing suburban community. Most of the adult membership has education beyond high school. They are employed by electronics firms as engineers, programmers, or are salesmen. Most of the congregation is white, but there are many minority groups represented in it. This church added 47 members within one year's time (mostly by profession of faith and baptism). The Sunday School is utilized as the primary outreach agency. An effort is made to keep the program as simple as possible and within their capabilities to staff them. Here, too, the pastor seeks to keep the importance of personal witnessing "everywhere to everyone always before the people." (Report received from the pastor, Allen Barnes.)

In addition to rather remarkable Sunday School, Training Union, Woman's Missionary Union and Brotherhood and Music organizations, the Hatcher Memorial Baptist Church of Richmond, Virginia, used special youth, senior citizens, and kindergarten organizations to help it grow from 1,772 members to

2,146 members in a two-year period. This church works intensely with teen-agers which they feel helps reach adults of all ages and fulfils a great evangelistic need in their particular neighborhood. The church also uses quarterly "fellowships" to break cultural and social barriers within the congregation.

This church is located in a declining area of Richmond and at one time was losing in membership at the rate of about sixty per year. With new direction in outlook and outreach, it is now growing. Churches do not have to die. (Report received from the pastor, John W. Patterson.)

Organizations and programs are just as important now as they ever were. The problem is that the world is not so readily brought inside the church house any more. The organization needs to be enlarged to admit the possibility of extending itself and the programs of the church out into the streets and into the midst of the needs and hurts of the world. As in the past, a major emphasis was placed on the educational program of the church, and this should be continued, making the educational program a ministering laboratory in which participants have an opportunity to demonstrate and tell who Christ is. Additional attention should be given to the use of small Bible-study groups in homes, or other places outside the church house. Flexibility in education should be sought so as to provide its helps to persons on differing levels of Christian development.

Communication and involvement are gained through *music* and *drama*. These early tools of the church need to be "rediscovered."

The music program of most churches is tailored to fit the appreciation of those who are already in the church, but it also should be adapted to attract those who are outside and who may not have the same level of music appreciation.

Churches have been known to argue, or even split, over the kinds of music used. This reflects an effort to "preserve" the church in a traditional mode. Strange how in many churches the organ is *the* instrument to be used. The organ, although excellent, is no more "biblical" than is a guitar; perhaps not so much so as a trumpet or a sackbut.

Church music has been too often confined to the church house. It needs to be used more flexibly in other places. Coffeehouses come to mind and these are often significant means of outreach, but usually present music on a "folk" level. Other levels can be reached as with small groups who like more classical music, chamber music groups, or choral groups.

A church in Johnstown, Pennsylvania, saw 130 conversions as a result of a music program performed in a shopping center and followed by intensive counseling and Christian testimony. Many churches are enlisting young people in church choir groups which may perform the new Christian folk musicals, and using these choirs to influence others for Christ.

Many churches which would not consider their church year complete without a Christmas or Easter pageant are repulsed at using this form of communication in other ways. Drama was developed by the early church and is a valid method of outreach today. Traveling drama might be used more effectively. Persons could be enlisted in the creation and performance of drama to depict a Christian thought.

Recreational programs are being used by many churches to attract and win people. Southern Baptists in Minnesota asked Al Worthington, a baseball great, to conduct baseball clinics in many areas. This he did, along with members of the sponsoring churches. At the conclusion of each clinic Al spoke of the "Great Game of Life and the Captain of His Team." Over 2,000 young people found Christ in one summer through this approach and backyard Bible classes which followed.

Crises significantly opens communication and involvement. All of those who have served as pastors of churches, or as laymen in a ministering capacity, have come to understand that a time of crisis in the life of an individual is a most appropriate time to communicate to him the meaning of Christ. Death and sickness have been special forms of crises which have attracted our attention. The pastor spends a great deal of time ministering to these needs. He has discovered that many contacts are made, that every time he ministers to a person or a family during these crises, he has ministered in a way to all those who know and love that family or person.

There are many forms of crises which manifest themselves nowadays. Our whole society is in a state of crisis. Here, again, it should be reiterated that in this is an opportunity for the greatest day of the church. It is because there are crises on every hand that we can best communicate. The world is in a state of crisis; our nation is in a state of crisis, as are our cities, our families, and even our homes. From the standpoint of communicating the gospel this is really an advantage. It is an advantage because people do not respond very well when things are going well. At a time when things are moving along pretty much as they have always moved and there are no real challenges placed upon them, people may not be too interested in finding a faith that is sure. They may have come to believe that if their family relationship is good, they have found the answer—that the family is the hope of the world.

If they are financially secure, they may feel that financial security is all that is needed. If the individual is in good health and has not lost a loved one recently, he comes to believe that all is well. It is when decisions have to be made; when roots have been disturbed; when the individual finds himself in a strange place; when no one seems to care whether he lives or dies, that he seeks an answer for his need.

It is when the alcoholic has discovered no way out; when the drug addict has discovered that he is without an ounce of hope that he is anxious to hear the *Good News.* It is when the inner city is disturbed with riots and is crying out in pain that it is ready to stop to hear the sound of peace.

In the book, *Church Growth and Christian Mission,* Eugene

A. Nida has pointed out that when crisis has been reached there comes a time of disenchantment and disillusionment.

Disenchantment and disillusionment may bring about disaster or even destruction. On the other hand, however, if at that moment of crisis when disenchantment and disillusionment with the old value of life sets in, a Christian can make his innovative move to provide an answer, then there is likely to be a positive response.

Should Christians and the church ever seek to produce crisis? Of course they should. This is what we are all about. It was what Christ was about. He was sometimes remembered as the "disturber." We are about the business of upsetting values in the lives of people who do not know Christ. We are concerned about disturbing the status quo. We ought to all be about the business of stirring up issues. We have *committed* ourselves to stirring up some issues. We like to stir up the conviction in a man that he is lost. We are a bit more reluctant, however, to stir up the conviction that Christians be the kind of Christians they ought to be.

It is said that Jonathan Edwards preached with such conviction that whole multitudes of people fell to sobbing and moaning with the very conviction that was raging in their hearts. Simply stated, he produced a crisis and that is a very good time to communicate.

Many churches have *specific groups,* or organizations, which do much to spearhead involvement for the church. They may be women's or men's mission action groups. Although they may have a larger responsibility in calling attention to world mission causes, largely away from the local church community, they likely are also interested in special projects which provide opportunity for involvement (and thus church growth) close by. For instance, they may provide ministry to elderly people, those in jails, literacy programs, juvenile rehabilitation work, and work with indigent people. Sometimes they may be the only group within the church which does much to call attention to needs of missionary call, commitment, and service. They may provide about the only incentive or motivation for outlook within the church. Sunday Schools, or classes, or a special missions committee often serve a similar function.

In the early development of the American church, it was the mission societies which spurred the church to growth and involvement in the Christian needs of the communities and the world.

Small groups have a real meaning to communication and involvement. In recent years these have given real impetus to church growth. Keith Miller, Robert Raines, and Elton Trueblood have caused us to consider afresh the usefulness of the small group.

The Lutheran Church of the Covenant, of Gardena, California, is using the small group to establish the church. It is an interracial, inner-city situation. The experiment is sponsored by the Department of Metropolitan Ministry of the American Lutheran Church and seeks new expression, structure, and worship, particularly in a highly mobile area. The pastor, M. Laurel Gray, reports, "Our main thrust is the small group meetings. We aim at adult adult education. The Sunday morning worship is a by-product, or spin-off, of what goes on in the small groups. It is planned by the people involved who also participate as much as does the pastor.

"Our entire structure and organization was planned by the people in all-day retreats held regularly. The pastor is an *enabler* to the laymen to help them realize and utilize their talents in all areas of ministry.

"The Sunday service is an attempt to carry this out. The worship part is short, designed to foster within the minds of people attending something about their own faith, which is then discussed in the adult feedback sessions. All adults are involved in this. The "Teaching Community" (Sunday School) is a cooperative venture in which all adults get a chance to participate on a revolving basis. The idea is to train all adults for their role as parents, teachers, disciples." (Report received from the pastor, M. Laurel Gray.)

The Faith Baptist (American) Church of Fort Wayne, Indiana, has experienced a growth of 253 members in two years in a suburban, professional type community. The pastor has led the church in the use of small groups to attain their growth. The church has no facility of its own, but meets in a public school building. (Report received from the pastor, Joseph Baker.)

Through the use of prayer bands, Bible study groups, in which there is a maximum *people* involvement, a Church of God of Hartford, Connecticut, has experienced good growth. Their pastor credits "the love of Christ" for the ability to break down barriers of race and need. (Report received from the pastor, Cecil Wiltshire, Church of God.)

The United Methodist Church of the Good Shepherd, Columbus, Ohio, grew by 121 members in six months, utilizing adult home groups for study, discussion, and witness. But to carry out the personal involvement completely, according to the pastor, *every member* of the church is a task force for specific needs. This church is well educated, young and old constituency being in an urban area of many apartments and single dwelling homes. This church also used a school building for its worship services.

The Oak Hills Baptist Church of Evansville, Indiana, has used Bible study groups in homes to implement a 300 percent increase in Sunday School growth in a four-year period.

In spite of great community change, the Albright Memorial Methodist Church of Washington, D.C., has used Bible study groups, visitation and personal witness, as well as a day-care program, to break down racial and economic barriers which would have defeated a less creative and purposeful church. The pastor has led in the promotion of many programs which involved the laymen and kept them optimistic in the confrontation with a changing community. The church building, valued at over one million dollars, was used, not only on Sunday, but every day of the week.

The small group can be used to build new churches, to feed older ones, and to break down barriers which may be caused by race, economics, image, or education.

Churches and pastors are often reluctant to use them because of the fear that they will detract from the corporate body of the local church. This does not need to be the case. Surely they must be kept *church centered and commissioned* by the church to perform a specific function for the church. Their creativity and growth will contribute to the whole.

It is important that the groups be changed, moved, divided, and/or enlarged from time to time in order to prevent inversion to the point that newcomers are either not welcomed by the older group or made to feel excluded because they have not been a part of the older group which has enjoyed many Christian experiences especially dear to it. But, of course, the church as a whole faces this problem.

Ministering as a means of personal involvement and communication has been dealt with to some extent as regards the Christian individual, especially in times of crises. There is a group or program dimension of ministry that needs to be considered further. Ministry can be the means whereby we are able to establish communication, perform a Christian service of alleviating suffering, and bear witness of him.

James S. Wright became pastor of the Highland Avenue Baptist Church in Jamaica, Queens, New York, in the early part of 1966. This church of sixteen members, which was hard put to continue its existence, met in a heavily mortgaged property which it had earlier bought from another denomination. At the time it had adequate physical facilities it did not have people to fill them. The pastor began his work with an understanding with the congregation that they would seek to minister to the surrounding community in every way they possibly could. Such a small congregation, however, was limited in the ministries it could perform.

The community was made up largely of apartment dwellers,

many living in high-rise apartments containing thousands of inhabitants. The pastor and his wife set out to discover what they could do with the resources which were at hand. While in the launderette one day, and noticing mothers with small children in tow, the idea came to them that the church might provide a place where mothers could leave their children while going to the launderette, or shopping, or to the beauty salon. Even their small church could provide members who would be willing to "baby sit" for a while. The program was undertaken to be in operation for two afternoons a week at the beginning. The response was so great, however, that ultimately this program was enlarged. Not only were children cared for, but families were reached. The pastor discovered that there were needs for counseling and made his services available. The "drop off" program developed into a nursery which Mrs. Wright operated with the help of other ladies of the church. The church began to grow. Other people were being enlisted and as soon as they were they became involved in a ministering program of some sort.

The community had in its constituency many people of diverse languages and nationalities. The pastor saw these cultural groups as being an opportunity for ministering. As soon as a family was reached in one of the language cultural groups, that family was utilized as a center or a bridge for expansion to the persons of his own group. Soon bridges were established to persons of Spanish, Korean, Japanese, Portuguese, and other backgrounds. This necessitated that the worship service of the church become multilingual. Jim Wright spoke only English, and he would say "that not very well." Persons with electronic ability built for the church a system for translation. Persons of the various linguistic groups were utilized as interpreters and the pastor could continue to preach in English while his messages were translated in five or six different languages. Then translation for the deaf was initiated.

The program of ministering now enlarged to include a coffeehouse and a youth hostel. These needs, as observed by the church, necessitated the purchase of a nearby apartment house which could be used for the youth hostel and the coffeehouse. The church had grown to such an extent that with the help of its sponsoring denomination it could purchase added property and continue to make sizeable payments toward the indebtedness it already had.

An opportunity arrived for the initiation of a Bible-study and youth program in one of the larger high-rise apartment complexes close by. A Sunday morning education program was initiated and followed by intensive visitation and ministry.

An opportunity for the purchase of a church house in the inner city of Brooklyn afforded itself and the congregation agreed to underwrite the indebtedness for this property. At this place many ministries were initiated with a youth program, weekday nursery program, drug addiction program, community involvement for benevolences, a literacy program, work rehabilitation program, educational program, a preaching service, and many other ministries. The Brooklyn work developed very rapidly and soon was organized as the Park Slope Baptist Church, having its own pastor to continue a ministering and evangelistic program of outreach. (Jarreal Buchanan and Larry Patterson were the first pastors.)

In the two settings in Queens and Brooklyn, lay persons were utilized to minister as they were able. Summer college student workers were employed by the sponsoring denomination to work with underprivileged and to carry on the various ministries of the churches. These programs would be enlarged to include programs of involvement in music and drama.

Highland Avenue Church was so rapid in growth that the church sanctuary was soon filled to overflowing, necessitating the church to schedule services at different times in order to accommodate the crowds. The weekday ministry enlarged so extensively that there was no longer room for it to be contained in the church house, so another apartment house was purchased. This apartment house of four stories, with considerable space, permitted the weekday program to expand on the lower two floors and the church continued to rent the upper two floors to help amortize the cost of the building.

After four years of operation, the church was actually reaching thousands of people in its field of outreach. It added over one hundred members a year who were new converts. This interesting intercultural, interracial church continued its outreach to the establishment of other chapels and ministries, such as that of the Utopia Parkway Chapel. Almost from its beginning this chapel set about to duplicate the program of the sponsoring church with weekday "drop-off" programs, educational programs, and worship programs.

A different type ministry is carried out by the Fort Dodge Urban Ministry, of Fort Dodge, Iowa. The project is a part of the Department of Urban Work, Board of Missions, United Methodist Church, Mission in the Valley. Its purpose is not that of building a local church, but to seek to enlist and coordinate the efforts of several churches of differing denominations in the area in the concerted effort to bring reconciliation to the inner city.

The program encourages those persons who become involved through the evangelistic programs of existing churches. It provides women's cooking and sewing classes, exercise, purchasing courses, clerical skills, interracial exposures and dialogues which have opened up awareness of problem areas and action in the area, such as housing, school problems, police and community relationships. The consultants have helped in developing minority group cohesiveness and provide a base of strength for community action and involvement.

While not subscribing exclusively to any singular form of biblical interpretation, its participants find themselves bound by a common conviction that biblical faith leads them to respond in concrete forms of action touching all dimensions of lives, as "faith action in love." They feel that God's creative activity continues through the action of his people in the midst of life, even though the consummation of his purpose may not be realized in their present time and place; and that the goods and materials of life are intended by God to be a means by which all men may express the grace-filled life as "man for others."

Therefore, it is the purpose of the Fort Dodge Urban Ministry to work with individuals, neighborhoods, organizations, political structures, and the basic institutions of Fort Dodge society to develop physical and spiritual wholeness for people in the Fort Dodge area, in which all persons have maximum opportunity for involvement and full participation ("Statement of Purpose," Fort Dodge Urban Ministry, received from Kenneth Fineran, Director, Mission in the Valley, Fort Dodge, Iowa.)

Many churches have been started by persons who are of a particular cultural group. This is especially true in our American day in which the population is so mobile, and some persons from one area of the country may find themselves in another area. They are drawn together by their culture and possibly by their denominational affiliation. Churches can grow by the utilization of such cultural groups, even though there is considerable opposition to the idea. There is opposition because somehow the fact that a cultural group comes together and wishes to grow its own church, reflects upon the churches which are already there. This should not reflect upon the churches which are already there, however. Those churches which are there are themselves established upon some cultural unities within themselves. They have grown accustomed to these cultural unities and do not really see them as being such. Those same congregations placed in some other cultural geographic setting would themselves perhaps seek to recreate the community which they have enjoyed.

The early church was built largely upon cultural identity. As groups of Jewish Christians found themselves in places like Rome or Cornith, or Philippi, they were an extension of their former cultural communities. Some churches have ruled out the use of culture as the means of communication and involvement. It sees to them undemocratic, un-American, maybe even un-Christian The reasoning, of course, is that the church is for everybody. Everybody is welcome to attend their church and if the presence of cultural groups is recognized by a special effort to minister to them there is the implication that they do not desire them to be a part of the whole. This should not be the case, however. It should be that because they have desired the cultural group to be a part of the whole, the church is attempting to speak to them in a language and culture which they understand.

This need for special ministering is especially great for persons who have recently learned a new language and are more familiar with an old one, or who do not understand the "way of life" of the community in which they live.

A danger that is faced, however, is that the cultural group becomes an end within itself, rather than a means of bridging the gap of one culture to another. Sometimes the cultural-Christian groups which are established become very exclusive so as to include only those who talk as they do, or are from the same place as they, and becomes inhibited in its own witness. Even if this cultural group may wish to witness outside its cultural community, it may have become so identified by its culture that it is unable to convince the community that it wishes to include it in its concerns.

Southern Baptist churches have experienced this danger within the recent years of their rapid expansion into new areas. They have found that although it was relatively easy to begin churches it was often difficult to make the churches become indigenous. New churches established had spent considerable energies in gathering people of their own culture and had thereby created an image for themselves that seemed to be exclusive.

Where there are language mission opportunities, it is discovered that when bridges are built to these cultural groups they often respond very quickly. The same is true where there is a ministry to be performed to the deaf, or persons of other identifiable needs.

Nonreaders are often drawn together by persons who are interested in teaching them how to read.

There are many different cultural, or subcultural groups, which can be ministered to by the church. Businessmen, secretaries, schoolteachers, farmers, migrants, fishermen, truck drivers are professional persons, of course, but, in a way they are subcultural groups. A church may be able to "bridge a gap" by establishing a ministry or outreach effort which is especially designed to communicate to a particular group, such as one of these.

4 Where Do Churches Grow?

Churches grow
. . . Where God is at work with people
. . . and in the midst of change
. . He works with all kinds of people
. . . of all languages
. . . and races
. . . and—everywhere
. . He works with people as individuals
. . His presence is custom made
. . . and he speaks in concern about people who
. . . . are hungry
. . . . and poor
. . . or lonely
. . . or unjustly treated
He is concerned too, with
. . . the newly converted
. . . . and about their Christian service
And churches grow
. . Where Christians are seeking to know where God is at work
. . . and they are devising means to discover this as well as "people" needs
. . They visit
. . . and publish
. . . and telephone
. . Now and then, they reevaluate themselves to see what they are doing
. . Where Christians are committed to being partners with God in reconciliation
. . . and are ready
. . . and willing to *do* something
God does not need *all* his people to *do* the same things, because the objects of his searchings do not all hear alike

. . He needs some
. . Who are spiritually sensitive to worldly hurts
. . . and some
. . . who are sensitive to the spiritual needs of the hurting world
. . . and a lot
. . who are less critical of the ways in which God uses other people
in his partnership
of love.

In spite of the fact that there is much discussion and pessimism about lack of church growth, churches are growing. In every denomination, in every city, and in nearly every area of our country, there are those churches which are growing. Churches grow wherever God is at work with people. And God is always at work in some way with people wherever they are. God is at the front line of change and there are many changes which are taking place in American society. America has experienced much change in the last fifty years in the area of communication, transportation, and community. Much has been written about the changes which have taken place.

And, again, let it be reiterated, that because there has been such change this is a marvelous time for churches to grow.

The Presbyterian Church, U.S., has recently made a survey of new church members in the Synod of Texas. The major purpose of the study was to investigate reasons for joining the church given by adults, who within the last three years had become members of the Presbyterian, U.S. by profession of faith. Virtually all of the members in describing the circumstances under which they first began thinking of joining mentioned some circumstances which involved major change in their personal situation. For example, marriage, geographical move, vocational change, birth of children, going away from home to college or service.

The implication is that at such times the person is most likely to be open to an invitation to consider church membership. If churches could be alert and aware of such changes, using whatever channels are appropriate and available, then they might be more likely to be in touch with people at the "right" time. This does not mean that the church must assume a hovering stance, waiting to pounce upon a prospect in his hour of crisis, but it does mean the church must be available and sensitive to minister in times of personal change in order that the experience will be a natural means of relating the church's message and life to the needs of the person. (Pamphlet, "Why People Join the Presbyterian Church, U.S.," Survey of New Church Members in the Synod of Texas, Synod of Texas, Presbyterian Church, U.S., P.O. Box 4428, Austin, Texas 78751, received from James W. Newton, Director, The Presbytery of Northeast Texas, 4309 North Central Expressway, Dallas, Texas 75205.)

Needless to say God is at work with all kinds of people who speak all languages of all races and in all kinds of places. He works with people as individuals and is concerned with specific needs of individual persons.

Although these are facts that we accept quickly, sometimes our churches do not act as though they were facts. It may be that many church programs and ministries of outreach are carried on as though people were all of the same language or race or lived in the same kind of place. Because people are different, churches must make every effort to communicate themselves in terms of the people's understanding.

Even in the same localities, people are not developed to the same spiritual level of understanding. It may be that a person's hunger, or the cries of the hunger of his children are so deafening to him that he is unable to hear God's "I love you." If the church seeks to reach him but is only able to speak to him in terms of the well-fed middle class, that church cannot possibly grow. Here it can be seen that church growth can be measured in terms of ministry, that is, in terms of how the church ministers to the human physical hunger of an individual. After the individual's hungering has been alleviated and he has seen the example of love and concern of the ministering Christian and his church, then he is likely to accept the spiritual witness. In the same way, the abject hopelessness of poverty may stop the ears of the individual's hearing the good news. But God is ready to speak redemptively through his church to the plight of poverty. It was when the prodigal son reacted from the plight of his dire poverty that he made his decision to arise and go to his father.

God is present and anxious to fill the hours of loneliness which exist in the lives of all people. Who has not felt loneliness? To some this experience is far more traumatic than to others. There is that frightful loneliness in the midst of many people in vastly populated cities. There is the isolated loneliness of the rancher and his family, or the loneliness of the schoolteacher who works with the Bureau of Indian Affairs in Sungnak, Alaska. But, God is present in loneliness and waiting to be joined in a creative work by some Christian who has a compassion for those who know loneliness.

In every community there are those who suffer the stinging hurt of injustice. A rage wells up within him. He is unable to hear a rational voice until the injustice has been dealt with. That is the level of his need. His neighbor may have passed this stage, or not yet have reached it. But he is on that level of hurt, and some Christian who is sensitive to injustice, some church which is ready to right the wrong of inequities of law or social or civil behavior, can act now and speak. A church can grow when it becomes able to speak on the level of man's understanding.

In every community there are those who are at the level of Christian conversion. This is also a place where God acts and where God speaks. It is a beautiful point in God's plan for man, but it is not the end of God's plan for man. The new convert may be the most likely person to communicate the experience of conversion to those who have not quite reached this level. It is interesting to note that in the survey made by the Presbyterian

Church, U.S., in Texas, it was the new members who were most likely of all the members of the church to tell someone else about their conversion experience. Churches grow then as they encourage these new church members to witness to others who are at the "conversion level."

God is at work with people who are of the level of Christian service. There are many people in every community who are on this level. They hold membership in different local congregations. They have an affinity one for another and are anxious to serve. They need to be shown how and where to serve.

Churches grow where Christians are seeking to know where God is at work and are devising means to discover his workings. To put it another way, churches are growing where they are actively trying to find the doors which have been opened by the Holy Spirit and are improving upon their capabilities of discovering where God is at work.

Every Christian and every church is equipped with some means for discovering the open doors. Some Christians (and sometimes, churches) have an acute spiritual sensitivity. There are many people in our churches who have long sought to find the needs of people so they could minister to their needs. These people have developed an acute sensitivity and are able to share in the needs often before they are ever voiced. There are others who have such a sympathetic understanding of needs that they are able to communicate a kind of empathy which makes their ministry most effective. Such persons as these are able to discover perhaps all the needs they will ever be able to minister to without utilizing more formalized approaches for discovery.

There are means for discovery which are "step by step" processes. These are organized efforts to discover needs. Churches which are growing are working at finding out what the needs are. That is, where is God working? On what level? With what people?

One of the most notable methods used by growing churches is that of personal visitation. Sometimes this visitation is almost totally carried out by its pastor. Churches often leave too much of the visitation to the pastor. But the conscientious pastor spends a great deal of time in visitation. Most often this visitation is directed to a known need, that is, the person is sick, or has made an appointment for the pastor to call. But quite often the visitation is not carried out to meet a known need, but to discover a known need.

James S. Wright, pastor of the Highland Avenue Baptist Church, Jamaica, New York, tells of an experience when he desired to discover if it might be possible to find people's needs by casual visitation. He would select a block, or blocks, of houses, or groups of high-rise apartments and simply knock on the doors, introduce himself and see if he could discover a particular need to which he might minister in the name of Christ. For one week he put aside all of his other responsibilities and did this very thing. Upon two occasions he recounts he was greeted at the door by people who were in tears because of some pressing spiritual need and who were responsive to his ministry. By the end of the week he had discovered fifty-five people of spiritual need who were willing to meet with him in a worship service in which the search for faith might be started.

In other instances the whole church (or as many of the members as will respond) may be enlisted in a house-to-house canvass, in which every home in the community is visited and a specific effort is made to determine the needs of the people of the household. This effort is usually more successful in smaller communities where the "trust level" of strangers knocking at the door is relatively high. Invariably the procedure discovers a great many needs and when the needs are discovered they are related to the church as a whole. The church then seeks to meet the needs which have been discovered.

Many churches have a special night for visitation. There are particular organizations of the church which have a responsibility for gathering at the church for prayer and then dispersing to the objects of their visitation in the community. Usually these persons to be visited are ones who have shown some interest in the church by attending the worship service or possibly by calling the church office. The church which is growing, however, goes beyond those who have actively expressed interest in the church to those who do not as yet know they need to have an interest in the church. This need for the church is pointed out. The church seeks to communicate its resources.

One means of discovering needs which has been employed by some churches, or church groups, is that of simply advertising the availability of its services, by use of mail-outs, newspapers, radio, and television. The Seventh-Day Adventists use this means very effectively. They advertise Bible-study courses in the local newspapers. In a little booklet, *Churches Come Alive,* which is compiled by the lay activities department of the General Conference of Seventh-Day Adventists, Robert H. Pierson recounts how a Bible school in the Southern part of the United States placed a three-line advertisement in a local paper offering open help to those who telephoned their number. In seven and one-half months' time, by actual count, more than 75,000 people listened to a recorded message and more than 11,000 enrolled in a Bible class which was offered. (Booklet and report received from Adlai Albert Esteb. Booklet published by Review and Herald Publishing Association, Washington, D.C., 1969.)

In Lancaster, Pennsylvania, a church of another denomination advertised in the paper the availability of its pastor for Christian counseling. Hundreds of people availed themselves of the opportunity of this service and many of them were brought within the sphere of influence of the church. Although the church had simply sought to extend its ministry in discovering needs, it found itself growing because it had sought to be a blessing.

There are many people who will respond to the possibility of remaining anonymous by answering a written advertisement, or in writing to a box number. Later on as they are assured of the good intent of the person, or church, to whom they are writing, they are more willing to become personally identified.

A more formalized means of discovering the people needs of the community is that of a religious survey. There are at least two means of doing this. One of the methods is by telephone and the other utilizes a house-to-house visitation with a census-type survey.

The survey by telephone is being used more and more, particularly in the urban areas. The main advantage of the telephone is that more people can be reached. It is easier to enlist persons for telephone canvassers that as door-to-door visitors, and each canvasser on the telephone can reach about three times as many people in the same period of time. The canvassing project is not primarily witnessing, but is an effort to locate unchurched people so that a cultivative program of witnessing can be directed toward them after the survey. The Home Mission Board, SBC, has developed a comprehensive guide for an urban church survey. (*The Urban Church Survey Manual,* Department of Survey and Special Studies, Home Mission Board, SBC, 1350 Spring Street, Atlanta, Georgia 30309).

It is suggested in the survey manual that the greatest need of many churches is a large, active, up-to-date prospect list, and a greatly expanded visitation effort. Many churches do limit their visitation to their own sick and absentees, and to persons who occasionally visit the services. These churches then wait for the unchurched people to call or to visit their services before the church initiates any contact with them. A more aggressive visitation is needed.

The survey manual further suggests that before beginning the survey the purpose for the survey be considered as well as the population and geographical area to be covered and the number of canvassers to be recruited. In light of the purpose, needs, and resources then a survey strategy is developed.

There are distinct advantages to the telephone survey as has already been mentioned. The telephone canvasser can reach more people than a house-to-house visitor. Additional advantages are that the weather does not hinder the telephoner. The telephoner can get into apartments and trailer parks and other places that a door-to-door visitor cannot penetrate. People will come nearer to answering the telephone than the doorbell, and if the proper procedures are utilized the canvasser can obtain as much information on the telephone as by a personal visit, and this information will be accurate.

When a telephone survey is utilized a special telephone directory needs to be obtained. This would be a directory which lists street addresses as well as the name of the resident.

Many churches, particularly in small towns or open country, are able to properly use a census-type survey which does utilize house-to-house visitation. There are many churches in rural areas which maintain an up-to-date religious census of their total area. In these instances the churches have made a house-to-house canvass and then have prepared a large map showing the roads, streets, and the houses of the people of the community. This map is maintained at the church house. "Survey captains" are assigned blocks of the canvassed field. These captains have the responsibility of maintaining the religious information in their area. For example, if a house becomes vacant and another famly moves in, the survey captain immediately calls on the new occupant, welcomes them to church and gets the religious information for the survey form. This information is recorded at the church office. It, of course, is a very comprehensive type of survey and a very valuable one, however, it is impractical in most of the densely populated areas in America.

The discovery of the needs of people of the community must always be preceded by the church's intention to do something about these needs. As has been stated before, there are many churches and many Christians who have never really committed themselves to being partners with God in reconciliation. They do hold theological truths, but they have not been motivated to an action as a response to the theological truth. The church cannot, and will not, grow until there is an adequate imperative on the part of the church people to discover needs and meet needs. This sometimes can be accomplished by an overt effort on the part of the pastor or some leaders of the church to lead the church in a restudy of their theological orientation and their mission to the world. This restudy may be accomplished by use of small study groups within the church. Small groups may also be assigned activities or special projects for investigation. Such as, the needs of the residents of a nursing home, a children's home, or the needs of people in low-rent housing areas. Some denominations already have such small groups with mission action assignment and they need simply to be directed to the task.

As the church members are led in the discovery of the needs they often become burdened for meeting these needs and they will find resources for the task.

A pastor who wishes to get his church involved in a particular mission need may take a small group on a tour of personal investigation. Mission groups may become mission *action* groups by this process. It is much easier for any of us to become involved in meeting needs if we have personally seen those needs and perhaps have had someone more sensitive than ourselves to interpret these needs to us.

God works in the churches where his people are willing to do something with him. That is, not only do they know what needs to be done, but they are committed to doing something themselves. Churches which are made up of people who are willing to activate a mission task will be well supported by the same people for the total mission program of the church. Mission support for activities in foreign countries or in distant areas of the homeland are more likely to be supported by churches which are personally involved in a mission action where they are located.

We need to remember that God does not need all of his people to do the same thing for him. He needs his people to do those things which he has best equipped them to do personally. Two or three churches in a community are not necessarily divisive forces in the Kingdom and in the community. They are, in reality, groups of Christians who have different personalities, and, therefore, appeal to persons of different temperaments. One such church in a community may have a "high church" type group worship service while another church may have a more informal presentation in its service. Different denominations of churches may have different personalities. The two or more churches thereby inhabiting the community should work together in areas of mutual concern for the body of Christ, but regard each other as legitimate functions of that body as hands are to the body, or feet are to the body.

Also, within each individual congregation there are the members with differing abilities. There are some members who are quite sensitive to the world's physical hurts and they are very anxious to minister in the name of Christ. On the other hand, there are some church members who are oriented to a more direct Christian witness to the spiritual needs of the hurting world. These are both very valid and valuable abilities and they are also both very Christian. Therefore, persons of diverse callings and abilities must learn to be tolerant of each other in the performance of their tasks in the local congregations. It is most unfortunate that some of God's people spend so much of their ministry condemning the way in which other of God's people do what he wants them to do.

5 Churches Grow—in the Country and Small Town

Rural America and the Church
. . in 1776
. . and now
The rural church is historically mission-minded
. . and evangelistic
There are changes in the community in terms of
. . communication
. . and transportation
. . and sense of "community"
. . and movement of people
There are problems of leadership
. . and poverty
Many rural churches are growing
. . by forming fields of churches
. . or parishes
. . and by using Church Development Ministry
They are growing in
. . Missouri
. . and Colorado
. . and Mississippi
. . and Texas
Small town churches are growing
. . in Kentucky
. . and Nebraska
. . and Louisiana
. . and Mississippi

America has been rural for most of its history. In 1776 less than 10 percent of the population lived in communities larger than 10,000 population. Presently, it is estimated that less than 10 percent lives in rural areas.

This rural heritage has had much to do with the growth of the American church. Isolation caused by inadequate transportation and communication determined that every small community would have its own church or churches. This would be especially true of the southeastern part of the United States, for this is where most of the rural churches have been located in America. There are well in excess of 50,000 churches in this part of the United States.

Rural communities and churches have always been in a state of change. Never has this change been more severe than at the present time. The early changes which were felt were changes brought about by mobility and the migration west. Rural churches were the nurturing places for missions, revivalism, and education. The Great Awakenings in America were especially felt in the rural areas. The churches served to fan the flames of evangelism and to thrust growing lives of lay preachers into the frontier towns of the west. After a time, the fires of evangelism died down and the opportunity for missionary extension were diminished because of the heavy establishment of churches and church members in rural areas. The churches then gave their attention to organizational emphases and the support of worldwide mission causes. The churches sent missionaries to the countries of the world and to the unchurched areas of America. But these churches were concerned about ministry and education and benevolences. The churches, acting singly, or cooperatively, in associations, state conventions, synods, and conferences, established many of the first educational institutions that the communities had. They established preparatory schools, secondary schools, and institutions for higher learning. Their laymen became active in the encouragement to establish public schools and they were participants in the administration of these.

Hospitals and orphanages were established in all of the major cities and in most instances these were largely paid for by churches in rural areas. The rural churches have historically given of themselves in mission work and in a professional ministry.

At one time, over 70 percent of all Southern Baptist missionaries and pastors had grown up in rural churches.

The southern churches managed to keep their sense of missions and evangelism at a burning level by developing many church programs which would train their constituency in missions, evangelism, education, and, therefore, church growth.

Then came the advent of the boll weevil and the following economic depression. Family farms which had already been broken down by the succeeding generations were increasingly unable to provide a livelihod. The failure of the cotton crop and the resultant depression made the standard of living even more desperate. The families began to move away. First, the tenant farmers and the sharecroppers were forced to leave. Many of these were Negro. They moved into the industrial centers and quickly established their churches there. (In the Harlem area of New York City is one square mile where there are over twenty-five churches in which membership is largely made up of people from the South). Young people also moved away. If they were able to finish high school and college they found their livelihood in areas more promising economically. Gradually older people were left on the farms and therefore in the rural churches. Some of these, as well as other younger ones who had elected not to go so far away from home, moved into the smaller towns and smaller cities in their home regions. So the process of movement in America would begin on the farm, move into the larger town, to the smaller city, or to the inner city of the large cities. As people made their way up the financial ladder they might move again into the suburbs of the larger cities. Sometime they might even move back to the open country and commute to their place of work in the inner city.

One of the most significant changes in America is the sense of community which has always been so strongly felt in the rural areas. In the small community there is a great interdependency and mutual concern. Since every rural community was endowed with at least one church, the influence of this church permeated the whole of the community concepts. Sometimes it was difficult to discern what was the church community and what was the sociological community. This reflects favorably upon the significance of the church to its community. It would also have significance when the southerner moved from his community to an urban area, or to some place outside the south. It would sometimes be difficult for him to determine whether he wished to build a church such as he knew in the south, or whether he wished to build a community, such as he knew. Very often the significance of denominational differences which he had felt in the south were not so important to him when he moved outside that area.

Groups of southerners might come together to establish churches which might be Baptist or Methodist or Presbyterian. But the real adhesion within the church was often not so much the dogma of the particular denomination as it was the fact of the southern heritage.

Some would call these folk churches. Sometimes they were. But it is not altogether fair to say that they are, for they still bear a great sense of mission and evangelism and determination toward church growth. As they moved out of the southland and were planted in other areas, they grew very rapidly.

As an aftermath of the Second World War a reciprocal movement began in America. That is, Northern businessmen, with their families, began to move into the growing industrial areas of the south. These persons might also gather together to establish a church of the denomination which they had known in other areas. These churches would also grow very rapidly, due quite possibly to that dynamic created by the very fact of being "a minority." As a result of this, Catholicism, Mormonism, Christian Science and Jehovah Witness movements, and other religious groups extraneous to the south have grown very rapidly.

Rural communities, of course, are not limited to the South, but the vast majority of the rural churches have been located there.

The rural communities of America are rapidly improving from the standpoint of financial resources. There still remains areas of extreme poverty in the Mississippi Delta area and the Appalachian region which extends from Alabama and Georgia to New York. Rural communities are not always farming communities. They may sometime be mining communities, or be made up of people who make their livelihood in industry. Rural churches bear striking similiarity to each other regardless of what may be the mode of livelihood of the people who make up the community. Ordinarily the churches are quite conservative in theology. They believe strongly in what they preach. They have a strong sense of mission. And though many of their best leaders have moved away they still have leadership and many are growing. They are using many methods to accomplish growth.

Let us consider some of these that are growing and the methods they are using.

Where the population loss has been heavy and the loss of leadership has been great, some rural churches have been unable to provide continuing programs which are meaningful. Two or more such churches may combine their resources and form church fields. This makes it possible to provide a more adequate salary for the pastor. And it may make it possible for them to have a better program than they have ever had. Often one program is provided in the building of one church and another program is provided in the building of another church.

Some interdenominational efforts have been carried out along the lines of the fields of churches concept. One notable experiment was that of the Dale Hollow parish in Tennessee. In this particular situation, churches of different denominations in a depopulating rural area pooled their resources to provide for special programs for the benefit of all. The denominations did not yield their theological distinctives but simply pooled their leadership resources.

The Alanthus and Gentryville Baptist churches of the northwest area of Missouri, recognizing the need for a joint ministry adopted an agreement of cooperation which provided for a resident minister to serve as pastor of both congregations and set up a committee which served to coordinate the activities of the two churches and to counsel with the minister so as to provide a maximum ministry for both churches. This ministry provided for a morning worship service and an evening worship service in both locations, as well as a midweek prayer service. This joint program kept one church from closing and gave to the other its first full-time resident pastor. Both churches benefitted from increased baptisms and finances.

There are some relatively new churches being established in rural areas. One of these in Yampa, Colorado, is in ranching country and only seven years old. This church is small in membership. It grew from sixteen to sixty-five in worship service, largely through an approach of pastoral visitation. The pastor seeks to live and work with his congregation. He gained a general identity with them, not seeking to preach "at" them, but to live his faith in their midst. This has been a productive ministry. The next step in this approach, of course, will be the development of the laymen to accomplish much of the visitation and ministry so that the pastor can serve more largely in an equipping relationship. (Report received from the pastor, Bobby Parker.)

The Rock Hill Baptist Church of Brandon, Mississippi, is an open-country church located ten miles south of the small county seat of Brandon, Mississippi. The membership is composed largely of farmers. There are some who work in factories in the city of Jackson (about twenty miles away). Educational level is that of high school, or less. It is a quiet, stable, predominately white community, often slow to respond to change. This church also is a part of a church field. The pastor commutes twelve miles twice a month, on the first and third Sundays, to serve another church at Puckett, Mississippi, for an early morning (9:45 A.M.) service and a 6:15 P.M. service in the evening. This permits full-time preaching services at Rock Hill and a resident pastor for both fields. Both churches are growing and provide a comfortable living for the resident pastor. The churches make use of Bible study groups and prayer groups, as well as personal visitation to accomplish their growth. In writing regarding the growth of the church the pastor remarked that rural churches often have to make adaptions in teaching methods and materials because the denominational programing is often directed toward larger congregations.

A rural pastor must be flexible and ready to adapt methods and materials to meet the needs of his people. Patience is a needed virtue. Rural churches respond slowly to change. They need to understand change; then they will respond. They must first be led to see the needs of their community before they can develop any concept of the spiritual needs of the world. The mission giving has increased in direct proportion to the response of the church to the needs of the immediate community.

Rural churches are no longer poor. They may be declining in membership, but they often have great financial capacities. Farms are no longer small. They are big business. The standard of living on the average farm in this community is better than the average city factory worker. Rural churches are not generally glamorous fields of service perhaps like pioneer missions. They are often discouraging and heartbreaking. It takes time to establish the confidence of the people in a pastor. The pastor must demonstrate love and patience while, at the same time, he must lead his people to respond to the Lord's will and purpose for them. A pastor must be willing to evaluate his work in terms of years, rather than months. Then suddenly he can see fruits of his labor in the Lord's vineyard. (Report received from the pastor, Rev. Russell H. Naron, Rock Hill Baptist Church, Brandon, and Union Baptist Church, Puckett.)

Although the pastor serves two churches, they are two different fellowships with different needs and wherein the churches may not be flexible enough, or near enough, to merge, it is possible for one pastor to lead them into commendable growth.

The First Baptist Church of Troy, Texas, is basically a rural church serving people who live in an area of 144 square miles. The congregation is made up of teachers, hospital workers, nurses, laboring people, and farmers. It is of all social and economic levels. There is a strong conservative, missionary spirit in the church. It has evidenced a good growth (in a two-year period of time experiencing 68 additions to the church which has a membership of 335). The church uses traditional organizations to assist it in growing. It gives special emphasis to the outreach abilities of the Sunday School. It used the Sunday School enlargement campaign to help launch its growth. The Royal Ambassador organization, which is a mission program for boys, sparked a revival in the church as the boys were converted and their parents became interested in the influence of the church. (Report received from pastor, Douglas Beggs.)

Some years ago, a grant was made by the Sears Roebuck Foundation and the *Progressive Farmer* magazine to fund a program of development for rural churches. Texas A & M University and Emory University were very much involved in researching and producing such a program for development of churches. The Methodist, Baptist, and Presbyterian denominations of the south were especially interested in this development program. After a program was formulated and produced in theoretical form, it was given to the interested denominations for use in their own fellowships.

The Home Mission Board, SBC, set up a long-range rural church program committee which studied the format of the church development program and adapted it for their use in churches affiliated with the Southern Baptist Convention. This came to be known as the Church Development Program and has met with considerable success, not only in the English-speaking churches but in the Spanish-speaking churches in Texas, New Mexico, Arizona, and California.

The basic concept of the program is to lead a church to analyze its objectives, resources, and community. It seeks to provide guidelines for developing the church's resources, spiritual and physical, and to seek to minister to the community and the world. A guidebook for the church development ministry is produced by the Sunday School Board of the Southern Baptist Convention, 127 Ninth Avenue, North, Nashville, Tennessee 37203.

The Hebron Baptist Church of Sardis, Mississippi, is located in the open country. The congregation is made up of persons who make their livelihood in farming, although there are a few professional people, such as schoolteachers in the congregation. The church is an old and traditional community church which reported 237 members in 1966. In a two-year period the church had 81 additions to its membership and it used the Church Development Ministry as a springboard for action. It has a strong evangelistic program and gives considerable emphasis to Bible study. The church considers that its greatest area of growth is not in numerical membership, however, but is in individual spiritual growth. The church has grown in stewardship from a budget of $15,000 to $24,000 in the same period of time. It carries a ministering program in the county jail and in a home for the aged. Additionally, the church gives ministering emphasis to rehabilitation for juvenile delinquents and alcoholics. While the church growing an expected product of spiritual growth was the calling of two preachers, a music director, and one person giving herself to vocational Christian service. (Report received from the pastor, James Jeffreys.)

Another growing church which has utilized the Church Development Program is the Emmanuel Baptist Church of Greenville, Mississippi. In a four-year period this church grew from a membership of 192 to 500. The church is made up largely of people who work in factories and some are stationed at an air base. The church is located in the heart of the Mississippi Delta on the Mississippi River. The church has a ministry in the jail, in rest homes, operates Bible study groups, and carries out benevolent ministries. It has a radio program on Sunday mornings on which the Sunday School lesson is taught. The pastor has expressed his feelings that the secret of the church's growth is God's will being done in the life of the pastor, and the lives of the members of the church. It is his opinion that the Church Development Ministry helped the church to discover its opportunities and helped him as pastor to coordinate the church program. (Report received from the pastor, Robert Perry.)

Churches are growing in small towns. The Yellow Creek Baptist Church near Owensboro, Kentucky, is rather typically located in a small town which has been engulfed by an enlarging metropolitan area. The city of Owensboro has overtaken the small-town community. Yellow Creek Church had been a rural church for many years. Then it became a "bedroom" of Owensboro, although it is not in the city limits. The pastor describes them as people who are cooperative and responsive to the witness of the gospel. They are responsive to the program of progress and are "geared to the times and desire to remain anchored in the faith." The older members who have been in the community for many years have received a great number of new people coming into the church with open arms and a great sense of felowship. Many things have happened to the church.

The pastor credits a strong visitation program as well as the Sunday School and a stewardship enlargement emphasis for growth of the congregation. In a two-year period the Sunday School enrolment grew from 422 to 780, and the financial stewardship increased from $28,000 to approximately $67,000 annually. As a result of the quickened spirit and the advance of enrolment in the Sunday School, there were 175 professing faith in Christ and 143 transferring church membership to the Yellow Creek Church. In addition to this, 15 young people gave their lives to full-time Christian service. The physical plant of the building was enlarged and the church has grown in depth spiritually. In speaking of the Sunday School growth the pastor says there are three points which are emphasized. "Find them, fetch them, and feed them." The pastor sends the names of prospects to Sunday School teachers as soon as they are found and every new person who joins the church receives a communication from the teacher of the class to which the new member would belong.

The pastor spends a great deal of time with his laymen. He has used opportunities to take laymen (as well as deacons) with him while witnessing in visitation. The pastor has sought to make at least twenty-five visits to prospective members a week in addition to his regular hospital and sick calls.

The church keeps a perpetual census of its community. The church field is zoned and each zone is assigned to a person who is in charge of that area for maintaining up-to-date information. When a person moves in or out, the zone "captain" calls the church office and notes the change in resident.

A ladies "voluntary working day" is observed at which time the ladies of the congregation are invited to come to the church to assist in some of the office work, in visitation programs, and prayer. An emphasis is given to the development of the young people particularly in responsibilities for visitation. Sometimes there are as many as fifty young people who visit prospects on a visitation night. On one occasion of visitation a junior boy won a young man to Christ and upon another occasion a little girl won another girl. A strong emphasis is given to evangelism and two revivals are held each year. The pastor believes that church growth demands discipline on the part of the pastor, staff, and membership. And especially an abiding faith and sense of direction is required. (Report received from Billy E. Roby the pastor who had just resigned the pastorate.)

The First (American) Baptist Church of Scottsbluff, Nebraska, has a cross section of professional, laboring, and farming people, as well as college students and faculty from four local colleges. It is located in the Upper Platte Valley with farming as a major influence. Most of the members are high school graduates, although there are many college graduates too. The church received over 100 new members in a three-year period of time, and gives emphasis to fifteen "faith at work" groups, which involves 200 people of the congregation (which has membership of 400).

The church carries on a student ministry. It operates a ministry in the men's county jail, and a branch church for Spanish-speaking people. The church gives strong emphasis to lay witnessing teams. Many of these visit in church communities of the area.

Effective renewal has come through small personal group experiences of study and lay witnessing. These groups give special attention to evangelism, witnessing, and personal testimony. Not only has the presence of these groups sparked growth in the parent church, but the influence in surrounding churches has been phenomenal. Witnessing teams have visited other churches in South Dakota, Iowa, and Wyoming, as well as Nebraska. The lay witness groups are sparking changes in church school classes, youth groups, missionary societies and student work, the worship program, and outreach of the church. (Report received from the pastor, James E. Rowe).

The First Baptist Church of Winnfield, Louisiana, is a church in a small town which is nearly one-hundred years old. Until recently it had shown a gradual decline in membership and participation in its organizations. There are five other Southern Baptist churches in the area of 10,000 people and the city is growing slowly.

But in the last two years there have been over 200 additions to the church and the financial stewardship has progressed from $102,000 to $150,000 per year. The church is noted as having an exceptionally high spiritual quality. The music program and the church membership training program has helped to give the church a determination to grow. It uses rather traditional means of church growth, that is, an emphasis upon its traditional organizations, such as Sunday School, church membership training program, its music programs, and its missionary organizations. The leadership of the pastor has undoubtedly given a strong sense of direction for growth. (Report received from the pastor, Thomas Cox.)

The Start Baptist Church, Start, Louisiana, is located in a farming area and is a small village with a small local school. It is a growing area and the membership of the church is actively engaged in personal witnessing and visitation. Here again, traditional organizations were emphasized to accomplish an increase of 10 percent in membership in one year's time. (Report received from the pastor, M. J. Martin.)

The Union Hall Baptist Church of Brookhaven, Mississippi, is located in a small town where the average income is $5,000 a year. It experienced a 25 percent membership increase in the years 1968 and 1969, utilizing the traditional Southern Baptist organizations for outreach and a dedicated constituency. (Report received from the pastor, Leroy Tubbs.)

The First Baptist Church of Zachary, Louisiana, is located in a small town which is made up of largely industrial workers, many of whom are high school graduates. There are a number of college graduates as well. This is a small town which is suburban to a middle-sized city. The church directly supports three mission stations outside of its community and in the past seven years has started one local mission that has since organized into a church. The church established another mission fifty miles away in a remote area where the state penal institution is located. This latter work was established when it was learned that there was a need for work among the employees of the penal institution and others who lived in the area. The church bought land and built a church and a parsonage. Later the mission was organized into a church with the sponsoring church assuming the indebtedness on the church building and committing itself to pay $250 per month on the indebtedness.

One of the remote mission efforts sponsored by the church was that of assisting another church in Montana by contributing $125 per month and underwriting that church's indebtedness on its educational building. The pastor has contributed his time to lead the Montana church in two revival meetings and has taken laymen from his church with him each time. Upon two occasions, the pastor of the church in Montana has been brought to lead revival meetings in Zachary.

Another remote mission work of the church has been that of supporting a church in Rochester, New York. The Rochester work was started by one of the former members of the Zachary church who had moved to Rochester. The Zachary church was able to double its local membership in a five-year period of time by exercising a major emphasis on missions with a maximum involvement of the people in the congregation. An additional strong emphasis was given to the youth ministry with an outstanding music program and missionary involvement, not only in the local situation but in the remote mission experiences as well.

Members of the church family are consistently involved in visitation and a continuing emphasis is given to the Sunday School organization of the church. (Report received from the pastor, Wayne Barnes.)

Small towns are excellent places for churches to grow. It is true that churches in many small towns become inverted and refuse to grow. But often, with pastoral leadership which is optimistic, and with a membership committed to growing, the small-town church is able to grow where it is and to make a contribution to other churches and areas of need.

Small-town churches are often feeders of city churches and have an excellent oportunity for the training of Christian workers. The program of the church in the small towns is easily publicized. Usually there is a county paper and a radio station, or other means of complete communication, which gives the activities of the church immediate access to the total population. People are well known to each other and there are not the usual hostilities of visitation and witnessing as encountered in more urban settings.

The small-town church has an opportunity for maturing Christian leadership and in producing financial contribution to the various programs of this denomination as most likely its building facilities are pretty well completed and its membership is stabilized.

Church growth in the small town usually is accomplished by a widening interest in the spiritual life of young people. Many small-town churches have not responded to this need very well because of the traditional structure of the church and because of the way the church has historically communicated its message. That is to say historically the message of the small-town church is beamed more directly to the very young, the middle aged, and the old. This characteristic is not true only for the small-town church, but is also true of churches in many other areas.

Youth can be reached if a special emphasis and interest is expressed in reaching them.

6 Churches Grow in Suburbia

This is a much maligned place for churches to grow
. . but it is a much needed place for churches
. . . Most people live there
. . . and just because they have nice houses
. . . and are mostly white
. . . there is no need to neglect or not love them
God loves them.

True,
. . Those communities and churches are having their problems

But,
. . Many of the churches are growing
. . . they are growing in
. . . New Jersey
. . . Illinois
. . . Georgia
. . . Pennsylvania
. . . Indiana
. . . Texas

Suburbia is a relatively recent newcomer to the American scene of living patterns. It is almost as recent a phenomenon as high-rise apartment in the inner city.

Suburbia has received a lot of criticism. It is often referred to as the place where "white Protestants" live as brought out by Gibson Winter in his book, *The Suburban Captivity of the Churches.*

And it is true that there are many people who are white and many people who are Protestant who live there. It may be, however, that the ratio in proportion to the population is not much larger for whites or Protestants who live in suburbia than in some other parts of America. It is quite likely that there is as wide a representation of ethnic groups and of those who are other than white in the suburban area of the city as for instance in the open country, or in the small towns of America.

Suburbia is criticized for being snobbishly affluent. Most likely, there is considerable snobbishness and affluence in the suburbs. And, of course, there are many people who live in the suburbs who are neither snobbish nor affluent. They do not all live in single residences. Many of them live in trailer parks. An increasing number are living in apartment complexes around the outer edge of the cities.

The churches of suburbia are often painted as being grossly callous in their concern for the people of the inner city and for the people of the world. The interest on the building indebtedness of many of these suburban churches is larger than the church's gifts to benevolences or missions. The churches are criticized for having fled the inner city and for locating themselves in the area most competitive with other churches.

These accusations are often true. The churches have spent a lot for their buildings, but they have had to build at a time when building costs were ever spiraling. Zoning requirements often made it necessary to build facilities with vastly expensive parking lots. In suburbia, with its restrictions, it often was not possible for the church to find "just any place" for the church to meet. There were no vacant buildings, no auditoriums to be rented. Likely, most of the school buildings were already occupied by other congregations seeking a breathing spell and financial growth in order to construct their building.

Most denominations have shown their greatest growth in suburbia. Theoretically, this would be where the churches were most competitive if all denominations were showing their greatest growth in suburbia. But, then, suburbia is where most of the people of America live. It cannot be denied that suburban communities and churches do have their problems. Every suburban community has its problem of communication, transportation, educational facilities, postal service, sewage, and of utilities. Its biggest problem, however, is with its sense of community. This is true of every type of community in America, but it is more keenly evidenced in a suburban community. Here America's population is most mobile, transient, and recently located.

Cleavages are poignantly obvious. There are the natural and man-made physical cleavages, such as rivers, hills, valleys, highways, and railroad systems. Man-made cleavages often were not really planned but just happened as the community grew up and expanded, as explained by Murray H. Leiffer in *The Effective City Church.*

Calvin Miller, who is pastor of a rapidly growing new suburban church in Omaha, Nebraska, observes the personal cleavages that exist in the suburbs. These cleavages are such as:

1. The well-paid common laborer versus the poorly-paid professional junior executive but live side by side.
2. School district A versus B in the same suburb.

These conflicts may be in friendly athletic rivalry, or heated issues of educational tax funding. (They may even be modular scheduling in high school versus the traditional curriculum scheduling.)

3. The suburban apartment dweller versus the individual homeowner.

Mr. Miller notes these cleavages being damaging because they introduce them in personal togetherness in surburbia. For example, John wouldn't consider asking his fellow car poolers to dinner in his home, or to the church for that matter, for, after all, his office is two feet longer than theirs and his salary is better; they are seat-belt buddies, not dinner partners (or fellow church members). In some ways the impersonal nature of suburban life causes churchmen to withdraw safely to their own side of the cleavage and stay there. The idea of witnessing to the iron worker across the street may be unthinkable to the college professor (who may be harboring some secret resentment because his house is not quite as nice as the iron worker, nor his salary as high).

Cleavages within the physical community are deterrent to close fellowship within the suburban church, and therefore makes it difficult for the church to accomplish its sense of community. On the other hand, in view of the same cleavages which are felt in the secular community, and the fact that the church has an adhesive (Christ) which the secular community does not have, the suburban church is often able to accomplish a great *koinonia,* or Christian community. It is an exciting new form of Christian community in that it does not run so great a risk of becoming a cultural or a folk church as did its predecessor which was a church made up largely of people who made their living in the same occupations and whose knowledge and interests were so very similar.

In spite of all the criticisms which have been heaped upon the suburban community and its church then, it must be seen that everything about the suburban community and its church must not be disparaged. Suburban churches are growing and they are giving support and concern to missions and witness and growth. Although they have been a bit remote from the problems of the inner city, they are becoming increasingly aware of these problems and many churches are acting responsibly toward meeting needs. (Paper prepared for delivery at Missions Class, Southern Seminary.)

The Haddonfield United Methodist Church of Haddonfield, New Jersey, is an example of such a church which is acting responsibly, not only in its community, but the inner-city community as well. This church has added over one hundred people a year for the past ten years and has carried on a remarkable program of ministry in the inner city of Camden, New Jersey.

The community in which the church is located is made up of upper middle- and middle-class persons, many of whom are professionals and businessmen and a large number of college graduates. It is located in the Jersey suburb of the Philadelphia metropolitan area and in an area which is basically theologically conservative.

In an article by Newman Cryer, which appeared in the October 1969 issue of *Together* magazine, the story of this great suburban church was told as to how it carried out its mission in the declining tension-ridden inner city of nearby Camden (a part of the metropolitan Philadelphia complex). Relying upon the leadership of the minister of missions, the Rev. Stanley J. Menking, the resources of the church were channeled in support for the people of a particular neighborhood of Camden. The church "adopted" the whole Pyne Point area of Camden. The essence of the urban ministry in Camden is that of the utilization of laymen who, out of Christian conviction, give their time and skills to upgrade the adopted neighborhood. In the inauguration of this ministry a series of urban encounters were organized with the aid of the mayor of Camden and other city officials and civic leaders.

Retreats were held using small group techniques and seminars. Laymen from the Haddonfield church utilized the knowledge gathered in their occupations, hobbies, and training to establish day-care centers in church basements, to repair old row houses and to work with the community council in the establishment of an employment service, a police community relations program, a block leader's organization, a biweekly newspaper and a summer recreational program.

As could be expected, the involvement of Christian laymen in meeting the needs of people in the inner city would reflect itself in the community in which these laymen lived and in the church which was the "launching ground" for their endeavors. The church is a dynamic one, growing in every area of its expression and adding a new dimension of Christian service to that of witness. (Report received from the pastor, Rev. Stanley J. Menking.)

The Westminster Presbyterian Church, Des Plaines, Illinois, is an example of a suburban new church development that found itself through accident and through choice on a hard path of slow growth. Its history raises some important questions for all churches to consider; what is the cost of faithfulness, and what is its effect on the community and on the church itself?

The church started with a traditional approach to church growth, utilizing many of the techniques and methods which had been developed in the 1950's and which were not working well in the 1960's; especially when the pastor and people were also determined to follow their understanding of what is required for faithful commitment.

Some of the church growth problems stemmed from the population shifts which had been unforeseen and which brought many more "non-Protestant" and more transients to the area than had been expected.

They abandoned the standard calling program in favor of an active program that got attention in other ways. They reorganized the "Session" into committees corresponding to actual function, that is, worship, training, action, and business. They started house-church groups for more intimate fellowship to sustain and train members for even more action.

But the church's insistence on standards for faithfulness also affected its growth rate as it required new members to take an intensive training course and there is a climate of opinion, if not an actual rule, that insists that every member spend time and money on church and community affairs and attending worship.

The apparent result of this attempt to practice what is widely preached is that the congregation stays small and poor. However, the church gets an unusual amount of attention and is able to contribute far beyond its numbers, both in its community and in its Presbytery. Outsiders attribute this impact to the church's being all of one mind and cohesive (although the congregation notices tension from within, it is not visible from without and there is an enthusiasm about the general direction of the church).

In a report made by Grace Ann Goodman, with the Institute

of Strategic Studies, Board of National Missions, United Presbyterian Church, USA, Miss Goodman observes that "some churchmen feel that action is only possible within such a small cadre; they resist growth fearing it would stifle creative action. Others say growth is not bad, but that a reputation for action will limit the number of those who are willing to join to a very few, although very solid, new members each year. In a mobile society, losses may even outnumber gains in any one period, so that the struggle for actual survival is never far from the surface."

Des Plaines, Illinois, is one of the long-established suburbs to the northwest of Chicago, and like other suburbs it went through a period of rapid growth after World War II. Farming land suddenly sprouted $30,000 homes; later shopping centers appeared, becoming focal points for the new communities. One such area was on the western edge of Des Plaines, both within and outside the city limits. In the unincorporated area a private development was built with the purpose of staying independent of any government (although it cooperates perforce with existing school, fire and water districts from several nearby towns).

The Elk Grove and Maine township line split the area down the middle and lack of any central focal point has fragmented residents into three parties for purposes of school boundaries, and two for other governmental services, such as fire and sewers. Thus, the area typifies much that is suburbia USA. Nearby industry brought in transient labor who needed short-term living accommodations and, therefore, apartment buildings sprang up rapidly. Ninety-nine percent of the population of the community is white. There are a few Orientals, but no Negroes. The age range is 81 percent in the 25–44 year bracket and the median length of residency in a single-family house is 2.9 years, and in the apartments it is 1.8 years. More than half the adults have completed high school and almost one quarter have completed college.

Religiously, 79 percent of the population holds membership in some church. Fifty-three percent of these are Roman Catholics in houses and 48 percent in apartments. Forty-seven percent of the Protestant population lives in houses and 52 percent live in apartments. Less than 1 percent is Jewish.

Westminster United Presbyterian Church found its beginnings in mid-1950 when the Presbytery of Chicago decided to buy four acres of land on the western edge of Des Plaines. The Presbytery bought a manse and called a pastor to found the church. He followed standard church development patterns of that day, calling door to door to locate persons interested in a new Presbyterian congregation, gathering them into house-size groups for further discussion and forming an Interim Council. On Pentecost Sunday in May, 1961, the Westminster United Presbyterian Church of Des Plaines was officially constituted with 57 charter members.

From the start the pastor had very definite ideas about how a new congregation should develop. Many of the charter members were inexperienced in Presbyterian ways and so the first basic demand was that everybody should go to a six-session membership course. The second was that for every two dollars spent locally a third should be designated to the denomination's mission budget. It can be seen that in this beginning the pastor was establishing a basis of faith and an outlook which would carry itself beyond the rather traditional ingrown attitudes so prevalent in many suburban churches. It is true that many of the prospective members viewed this stance as one that demanded excessive zeal and so they simply dropped out of hearing them. Others "took the plunge" generally coming up with the surprised feeling that this was a rather good thing after all.

Membership classes were scheduled three nights a week and no excuses were accepted for failing to complete the course. Long-time Presbyterians were a bit insulted at being asked to take the membership course and some of them refused to join the church on that account. But, on the other hand, there were those who would later report they "didn't know what church life or Presbyterianism was until they came there." The heavy giving for mission causes raised some eyebrows but people were loyal enough to their pastor to give it a try.

After the membership courses were over many of the people found they missed both the small group fellowship and the actual study and asked for Bible groups which were formed. The only formal activities of the congregation, besides the Session and committees, were the Sunday morning worship, Sunday School, Bible study in homes on week nights and a monthly family night supper at the manse basement (which the men furnished into an all-purpose meeting room with an outside entrance).

The new congregation's growth was slow, far below the Presbytery's New Church Development Department projections. In the first year, 1962, actual growth was 26 new members; 37 joined in 1963; 20 in 1964; 18 in 1965; and 13 in 1966. Part of the reason was an unanticipated transiency, and (possibly) the reputation that the church required a great deal of participation on the part of the membership. The members who joined reported a growing feeling of commitment and exhilarating sense of joint purpose and fellowship. The church became known as one which had a distinctive, alert, open congregation with more of a sense of missionary orientation than usual.

The church became actively involved in its community and in community issues. Members of the church became involved with migrant aid, child care and summer camping programs, as well as health programs. Each year the elders took on a project with some needy family, sometimes a Spanish-speaking migrant worker in need of housing, food and clothing, and health care, etc. The church was also involved in resettling Cuban refugee families and provided them with a start in the Chicago area. A study group, with the church's approval and interest, got the idea of trying to link up with an inner-city church for mutual education. Eight couples from the Westminster fellowship met monthly alternately in Des Plaines and downtown. Informal conversations were established and an informal study of a theological text were initiated. Later, after meeting very profitably together and establishing good relationships, the meetings were discontinued due to the heavy pressures on the young families involved.

In 1963, the congregation set about to build a church house. This building was completed and dedicated in September of 1964. It was a one-story building, with the sanctuary seating 175. It had a small electric organ, space for the choir in the rear of the sanctuary, rather than in the front. It was conceived as the first of three units and included an office for the minister, rest rooms, a couple of rooms for the nursery, and classes, and one room containing a small kitchenette.

As with many new churches, the presence of the new building attracted a few new members who had been holding off to see what it would be like. And for a time the congregation was delighted. Then, later they began to realize that there were some limitations to the new plant and possibly that the accommodations of the schoolhouse in which they had earlier been meeting was more adequate than what they had managed to build. Additionally, there were the heavy finances required for owning their own church house (although the indebtedness of the little congregation was not as large as is felt by many such suburban churches). Membership grew, as did the congregation's concern for missions. At this point it set about to rediscover itself, to determine really what was its direction to be and what was its purpose for being. In January, 1966, a committee presented for congregational approval the following statement of mission:

"Because God gave His Son for man the mission of Westminster Presbyterian church is to participate in Christ's redemptive, releasing, reconciling work in the world; to affirm that God is alive in the world; and to demonstrate by our lives that God created this work for all men."

"We felt the old structure was not good enough to do this

job—it was too inward looking," the committee chairman explained. Another committee members said, "We found that the building and raising the budget and such were taking so much time we had little left to do our mission. Also about 65 percent of the congregation was assigned to some committee and the kind of decisions they were making could be made quicker by a small administrative group. Lots of people don't really have time for committee work, so we now let those who want to do the work do it and don't worry about having some assignment in the church for everyone. I feel it is more important for the man that is on the school board, for instance, to spend his time there than on some church committee."

The new structure included four general committees for worship, training, action, and business. The worship committee was responsible for conducting the corporate worship. The training committee had a task "to teach how one commits his life to Christ," with specific responsibilities to set up principles, provide resources, materials, cultivate and train leaders, and plan and execute programs for Christian education of children and adults. This included special education on stewardship.

The action committee members had the responsibility of putting in concrete terms the relevance of the gospel to the world. It held a specific mandate to define community needs and organize resources to meet them; to develop community discussion of issues, maintain communication with significant community groups, and promote denominational mission programs. The business committee had the job of maintaining the property, handling funds, publicity, and office work, as well as maintaining personal responsibility lists.

In some ways the new committees were only new names for previous groups. For instance, the training committee represented the old Christian Education committee. But there were some significant changes. "Fellowship" was dropped from the old worship and fellowship committee because "we felt fellowship is engendered by a common work, not by social gatherings," the structure chairman said.

Action replaced evangelism and outreach as the congregation came to feel that the most effective evangelism was through action. An elder said, "When we called on people all we had to offer was an invitation to worship; sometimes the only real service that we rendered was to tell them where the bank was located."

The church is making a self-conscious attempt to find the pattern that will make the church make sense in the suburbs. "It is possible to run the risk of berating people for their affluence and not seeing them as people, with their aches and pains and joy and sadness," one pastor has said. In a proposal to the congregation he stated:

"Our community is no exception to the forces of change. In the affluence of suburbia we are easily lulled into a complacent apathy. Yet beneath the quiet surface lurk the haunting questions of the meaning of life and the responsibility of one person for his neighbor, whether that neighbor lives next door or in the heart of the city. In the midst of change the church is no longer a haven of safety with sure answers for bewildered seekers. The church is also changing and the direction of change is not always clear or acceptable to many. Traditional forms are labeled irrelevant by some while the concern for social involvement seems to overlook the importance of long-held symbols of religious meaning and practice for others.

"We understand the church to be that community which is called by God as we know him in Jesus Christ. To claim the possibilities of humanness for all men and to participate in the tide of history as those who give witness to love is justice and compassion. We recognize that the church is a sleeping giant chained to illusions of the past, afraid of the future, and more interested in survival than sacrifice. Yet we affirm that there is to be this awakened church in responsible decisive action within the world to accept a discipline of participation, learning, and concern, to affirm Jesus as the Christ for our model as the life-style of Christians today." (Report received from Gordon H. Skadra, Associate for Local Church Strategy, Board of National Missions, United Presbyterian Church in the USA, New York, New York.)

The experiences of Westminster Presbyterian Church are those which are felt by many churches in suburbia. Many suburban churches, however, may not have shown a depth of spirit and an objective concern for their purpose as has Westminster.

Wieuca Road Baptist Church of Atlanta, Georgia, is a good example of suburban church growth. It has grown from a mission chapel to a membership of 3,300 in sixteen years. In a recently completed two million dollar sanctuary, 2,000 attend Sunday morning worship; 1,500 come back at night. Those who come are of many different attitudes and ages. Young people flock to Wieuca, contrary to "drop-out" trends.

Wieuca isn't just traditional programs. Its members staff such activities as adult literacy classes; language classes for Orientals and Cubans; a program working with unwed mothers at a local home; a citizenship class; a tutoring project for poverty kids. "Our women pick them up and bring them to the church," says the pastor. "You can see them drive up in their Cadillacs with those little black children."

"Every Sunday two carloads of Wieuca members man a local mission, and women of the church hold sewing classes and serve food at another mission in the inner city."

Last summer a basketball clinic, which included black and white youth, was held in the recreation building.

Approximately one fourth of Wieuca's budget goes for missions, what the pastor calls "pre-evangelism activities."

The key to Wieuca's success is difficult to detect. Part of it may be the emphasis on missions. "We do more than sing hymns," says Bill Self, the pastor. "Outreach is important."

But more important may be the pastor's desire to create community, to build a concept of family among the diversity of a church. People retain their membership at Wieuca because "people love them."

The church tries to say in the midst of a cold and sometimes impersonal world, "We love you." The intangibles are emphasized. It can also be said that the pastor and the church emphasize affirmation of sins of loving personhood. The pastor feels strongly about a vigorous pulpit ministry, free of congregational pressures and prejudices. His sermons hit hard on such controversial topics as Vietnam, race, ecology, and sex.

But when the pastor speaks it is not to condemn, but to affirm; not to blast but to ballast.

Although many of the churches have staffs which are equally good, to quote the pastor again, "We've no easy answer. We do not discount the power of the Holy Spirit." (*Home Missions*, Home Mission Board, SBC. March, 1971. pp. 32–34.)

The Central Baptist Church (American) of Wayne, Pennsylvania, is located in a suburban community fifteen miles west of Philadelphia on Route 30. Its membership of 238 families comes from an area of fifteen miles radius from a church. The church has an annual budget of $136,000.

In the period of 1958 to 1969 it received into its fellowship approximately 600 new members. Its total program is a program of involvement in the lives of people. The pastor says, "We are not so much interested in growth as we are to enable this church to be an agent of change in the area, to the end that the community be appraised for justices done and love as seen in action."

The church involves itself in many forms of reflection, activity, and research. Bible study groups meet on Sunday mornings and during week-nights as well. There are open forum discussions.

The church budgets approximately 47 percent of its budget to missions giving. It has resettled five Cuban refugee families. It was a participant in the international Christian youth exchange program. It is active in fair housing programs and sponsors sewing classes and operates a thrift shop. It is a member of the Main Line Housing Improvement Corporation, works with alienated youth, operates an integrated nursery school, and participates in tutorial projects, as well as having contributed $100,000 to its denomination's missionary funds.

In order to adequately involve its membership in purpose and concern, its members are involved in research projects in north Philadelphia and has task forces operating in fields of public education, police relations, problem pregnancies, and prison reform.

Following the death of Martin Luther King, Jr., in April, 1968, the church established a Martin Luther King, Jr. memorial fund with a corpus of $100,000. The church mortgaged its property in order to do this and it used the money to provide the kind of programs in which the late Dr. King was involved. Specifically, to relieve the problems of inadequate housing, education, and employment in the Philadelphia area "to create a more just and humane society." A year later the pastor reported, "We discovered that the establishment of this fund was a tremendous education and evangelistic program for our church. We have learned about the whole metropolitan area and some of its needs. We have met many persons and have already become involved in other ministries through people we have met."

Ninety persons joined the fellowship during the year, most of them saying "We heard about the church through the King fund," or "We had given up on the church, but are now willing to look at it again." (Report received from the pastor, Richard Keach.)

The Delaware Valley Baptist (Southern) Church, Willingboro, New Jersey, has experienced a most unusual growth. It is located in the suburban area of Philadelphia, in a community of approximately 40,000 population, which is approximately ten years old.

As is true with many suburban communities today, it is totally integrated. Of course the church is too, and although only about one fourth of its membership is black, on almost any Sunday over one half of the Sunday School will be black.

The pastor describes the church atmosphere as being "evangelistic, informal, yet with good organization and friendly."

The church has averaged approximately 200 additions per year in the last three years. Almost one half of these have come as new Christians.

Although the church meets in a newly-constructed building, by the time the church house was completed it was inadequate to contain the growing church. A part of the church's program continues to be carried on in the schoolhouse in which the church itself recently met for its worship services. The church is very missions-oriented and it is quite evangelistic. It has as its goal the establishment of one new church-type mission each year. It has already mothered four or five new congregations. In the recent years of the rapid growth of the church the pastor attributes the growth to an adherence to following principles of growth; that is, discover prospects, expand the organizations, enlist and train workers, provide space, and visit. An effective use is made of publicity, promotion, and public relations.

This church uses an extensive bus ministry which has added much to the growth. Over one third of the congregation comes by bus. Many are young children, but there are more teen-agers who ride the bus than any other group. There are a few adults who would not have transportation otherwise and over one half of those who come to the church are Negro. But the bus ministry not only enlists many who never would otherwise be reached, it also is a good tool for ministry.

The church is very active in ministering. Each bus is assigned a lay "pastor." Of course there is a layman of the church who drives the bus, but the lay "pastor" moves about the bus while it is on its way gathering up its passengers or returning them to their homes and he inquires about their welfare, any home problems which may exist, and their spiritual needs. As could be expected, many doors are opened by this pastoral ministry on the bus. And as needs are discovered, it seems that the whole church responds as a body to attempt to meet this need. The ministering program of the church is on an individual basis. Members of the church may discover a need, whether physical or spiritual. They seek to meet this need and if it is not possible, they enlist other members of the church to assist them in the task. The church is a praying church and at almost any time groups of members may be found in the building in prayer for some specific object of their interest.

Although most of their ministering is person to person there are some formalized ministering efforts. One of these is carried out in the inner city of Philadelphia in the Kensington area. Another ministry is operated in a low-rent housing area. In addition to this the church operates a rescue mission. It has services on the boardwalk of a nearby resort area. It has a ministry at a naval hospital. It is one of the finest examples of a church combining witness with ministry.

In addition to its strong and unique ministering programs of outreach, it carries on traditional forms of organization, that is, Sunday School, Christian training, Woman's Missionary Society, Brotherhood, and church music organizations.

The Sunny Place Church of God of Bensenville, Illinois, is a young church which has recently doubled its membership in a three-year period of time. Its congregation is made up of middle and upper middle class, skilled tradesmen, white-collar workers and about one half of the congregation's adults are college graduates. Its members come from a radius of twenty miles and the pastor describes it as "having good social communication; as being progressive in theology and social awareness."

The church members are described as having a strong consciousness of a personal experience with Christ, although their witness is largely nonverbal. The church's members are concerned with community involvement.

The church is located in a highly mobile area into which many of its members have moved from all parts of the country. It has a strongly united fellowship which has held the membership together even though they may have moved farther and farther away from the church into another suburb.

New families have been added and many of these have been influenced as friends of families who were active in the membership of the church.

The pastor describes the greatest attraction to the church is that it has a highly open and contagious fellowship and has an unauthoritative leadership. "We have tried to be open to, accepting of, and helpful toward all sorts of persons." (Report received from the pastor, Robert Jack Smith.)

The Faith Baptist Church (American), Fort Wayne, Indiana, was organized on October 12, 1967. This American Baptist fellowship came about as a result of a study made by the field minister of the Indiana Baptist Convention and the staff of research and planning of the Indiana Council of Churches. The study revealed a substantial growth in northeast Fort Wayne. It clearly indicated the need for the establishment of an American Baptist Church.

The area within a three-mile radius of the church site had a population of approximately 30,000 people in 1968, living in approximately 8,700 dwellings. It was well supplied with shopping centers and schools. Twenty-eight churches served the area. When the Faith Baptist Church fellowship was constituted the charter roll consisted of 142 names, representing 52 families. An elementary school was used for weekly church school classes and morning worship services for the rental price of $50.00 a Sunday.

It was determined early in the history of the church that the church would be started and made to grow through the use of small groups. Although, of course, there were several factors that would help to make the Faith Baptist Church a success story, the strategy of establishing small groups proved to be a significant factor in the church's growth and development.

The pastor has written an interesting account of the development of the church in a brochure published by himself entitled, "Strategy for Mission Through Small Groups." When the pastor arrived on the field he started calling on those persons whose names had been given to him by a few members of the steering committee which had called him to this new challenge. The list included only three or four names, but when each of these families was contacted he would ask, "Do you know anyone who isn't attending church anywhere?" If he was given other names he immediately called on these people. Other prospects were made available by interested persons who attended a reception that was held for the pastor at the time of his arrival. American Baptist churches which were sponsoring the new work in Fort Wayne informed their members of the new effort and suggested that they were free to attend if they wished.

During the first 18 months, a total of 75 persons were added to the Faith Baptist Church from the four supporting churches. Of these 75 persons, 18 had been inactive members. Through house-to-house visitation the prospects who were discovered by many different means were gathered in a Bible study group in the home of one of the members. Within two weeks four additional study groups had been started. The pastor continued his ardent visitation and in one period of two and one-half months made 341 calls. These calls included new contacts and follow-ups. When the pastor visited a family and discovered interest in the new church he immediately asked them if their home would be available for five or six couples to come together at a specified time for the purpose of study and planning. The groups studied the mission of the church, Baptist beliefs, the church covenant and its relationship to Christian living, and the qualifications for church membership. Group meetings involved sharing of past religious experiences and ideas and dreams for establishing a church. No families were asked to make a decision in public discussion or private conversation as to whether they would become members of the new church. They permitted each couple to freely withdraw from the group at any time without embarrassment. No offering was taken in the study groups, but occasionally someone did make a contribution.

The first formal invitation to church membership yielded 32 couples who agreed to attend one of the five studying and planning groups. Two of the five small groups met on Sunday, one in the afternoon and one at night. The other three met at various homes at night during the week. Each group met for six sessions with the same agenda. Sessions ranged from one and one half to two hours and they included a refreshment and fellowship period. Each session was opened and closed with prayer. The study groups considered such things as their own available talents and their consideration of the mission of the church in the present time. These considerations were made early in the life of the small group meeting in order for the participants to see the need of the church to have clear and well-defined goals or objectives. The setting of goals was a joint effort involving both laymen and the organizing minister.

The second meeting of the small groups studied the Christian symbols found in Baptist churches, such as the cross, the baptistry, the Bible, the pulpit, the communion table, candles, flowers, offering plates, the Christian and American flags. It studied also the various forms of worship. The pastor notes that the second session proved to be a significant one in that all the groups had members whose religious orientation was much different from that of other members of the group. All members of the group found this to be a very helpful session.

Session three was a study of the Baptist covenant with preliminary work on a proposed constitution and bylaws and with job descriptions for the possible staff and officers of the new church. The traditional Baptist covenant was studied very carefully and partially revised and rewritten. All five groups eventually gave tentative approval of the final draft which was later incorporated in the proposed constitution.

The fourth meeting of the small group centered about a discussion of the question, "What does God expect of me as a Christian?"

Session five discussed the question, "What are the distinctives of the Baptist witness?" This meeting usually lasted a full two hours. The subjects of doctrine, local church polity, denominational affiliation, interdenominational relationships were fully discussed.

Session six discussed the question, "What will this new church expect of me if I become a member?"

Another set of five study groups was established for the purpose of learning about stewardship and particular stewardship program recommended by the American Baptist Convention.

After stewardship was discussed as relates to the Scripture, the needs for the new church, and the need for every family participating, commitment cards were given to each family represented. Both husbands and wives were asked to make their prayerful decisions at home and then return their cards by mail. All of the 33 families which had been involved in the five study groups returned their commitment cards with treasures totaling over $17,000. The proposed budget for the year was prepared on the anticipated income.

Upon discovering the success derived from the initial study and planning groups, the pastor decided to modify the contents used and to continue to employ the approach in bringing people into the life of the church. These groups were called "Adult Inquiry Groups" rather than new membership classes because it seemed desirable for each inquirer to honestly feel no obligation to unite with the Faith Baptist Church. As a result many couples entered into the group that otherwise might not have done so. Ninety percent of those who attended the group meetings eventually united with the church.

If a family indicated interest in the church as a result of the members or the pastor calling, then an invitation was given to them to enter an Adult Inquiry Group. These groups were informal, held in homes, and did not impose a psychological obligation upon the "inquirer" as a more formal setting might.

If the persons contacted were newcomers in the community, and in many instances they were, they were told that to participate in group study was a good way to meet new people and make new friendships.

Including the initial five groups, sixteen groups met for study over an eighteen-month period. As a result of these group meetings 86 families, or 221 members, came into the membership of the Faith Baptist Church.

The pastor observes that in the establishment of small groups there is no set pattern, but that the more simple the structure, the stronger the group. Flexibility is the key word as the group seeks to be person-centered. Persons should not be pushed in groups, and the small groups can be started by concerned and prepared laymen, or by a pastor. If the pastor has a leadership role in the groups beginning, then it needs to be clearly understood that the pastor will relinquish his role to lay leadership.

The pastor suggests some guidelines for establishing small groups:

1. A group may consist of four or five, or from four to six couples, or from eight to twelve persons who may not be related. Generally speaking there is greater interaction within the group when it is composed of persons not related to each other than when a group is made up of solely married couples.
2. A group ought to meet in the homes of participants on a rotating basis.
3. A group generally has refreshments which are provided by the entertaining couple at the close of each session.
4. A group determines the day, time, agenda, and length of sessions.
5. A group ought to meet at least twice each month. Some have found they could meet weekly.
6. A group meets for nine months, September through May, with the summer months being used for the training of new group leaders and growing inspiration, insights and assistance from the experienced group leaders.
7. A group may choose to meet regularly from four to thirteen weeks and then disband.

8. A group should be a face-to-face encounter group and consequently devoid of long speeches or lectures. The natural seating arrangement of a living room has proven very satisfactory. There are no observers or spectators. All are involved.
9. The group should have a leader who serves as catalyst. He is to encourage each member to share in the discussion.
10. A group leader is not to dominate the discussion.
11. A group should require of its participants discipline, study, and faithful attendance.

Although this church has used the small groups for the beginning and development of its new church, the pastor suggests that small groups may well be used by the church in ministering. Small task force groups might be established to engage in tutorial programs, a ghetto school, to conduct weekly parties for children at state school for the deaf and blind; to make regular visits to a nearby mental hospital; to visit school board and city council meetings; to gather, maintain, and distribute clean useable clothing to needy families in the community and city, or inner city; to chaperone weekly youth night in the community youth center, or inner city center; to visit senior citizens in homes for the aged; to establish and staff a church school class for retarded persons; to seek out the possibility of ministering to persons who are artists, musicians, playwrights; to develop and implement a strategy for mission to the mobile family.

In regard to the small group, however, the pastor cautioned that the effective group is the one which does not exist by and for itself, but its true life is to be found in the church.

(Report received from the pastor, Joseph L. Baker.)

The Tallowood Baptist (Southern) Church, of Houston, Texas, is located in a suburban area of excellent housing and schools. The membership is of high educational level. The church is strong in its outreach and has a warm spiritual disposition with strong lay leadership. This church extends its influence with the use of area coffees conducted by women of the church and as prospects are reached and they become interested in knowing more about the church, they are engaged in weekday Bible study groups.

The church operates several mission activities in the inner city with persons of other races and nationalities. Due to its very rapid growth, it has met in school buildings upon two occasions and for two years it was necessary for them to have three worship services on Sunday mornings. It has had two worship services for six years.

The church has largely used traditional church organizations as found in Southern Baptist churches. It has given a strong emphasis to its Sunday School organizations, its Christian Training program and to its music program. Women's and men's missions organizations have continued to promote a philosophy for local mission action. The women's organization has sponsored a ministry to foreign women. (Report received from the minister of education/administrative Pat Vickery.)

O. D. Morris, in an article in *Home Missions* magazine, March, 1971, notes that most suburban churches grow as a result of inherent homogeneity, but as the area matures into the polyglot of urban life, diversification is imperative. The suburban church must have a strong theological base which requires application as well as theory. This demands an accurate concept of metropolis in which the suburban community is recognized as only a part of a total community and therefore morally irresponsible unless it strives for a totally integrated metropolis.

The suburban congregation must strive for a wholeness to the Christian witness in every area and among all strata of society. The congregation must seek Christian solutions to the puzzle of urban living. It must enrich city life, rather than frustrate it by isolationism. The specific needs of the church and community provide the focus and shape for many forms of ministry.

The suburban church can, and most likely will grow in suburbia. Its responsibility, however, is not completed in the suburbs.

7 Churches Grow in the Cities

Cities of tomorrow
Cities of today are
. . centers of learning
. . seedbeds of change
. . and changing
City churches are growing in
. . Indiana
. . Pennsylvania
. . Florida
. . Alaska
. . California
. . Texas

The Journal of Insurance Information, in its *Report on Tomorrow, A Survey of the Seventies*, indicates that in the next decade many people who have the means of fleeing the city will do so by changing jobs, but the vast majority will be unable to flee. The problems of crowding, noise, traffic congestion, housing shortages, deteriorating services, and slums will continue to get worse and then possibly get better. Many solutions are being discovered to alleviate the problems so that the cities may become not only liveable, but perhaps even likeable once more.

It is anticipated that the urban population of the United States will rise to 80 percent by 1980. There will be a reconstruction of the inner cities by the construction of pedestrian malls, vertical cities within a city, and such other innovative improvements. Even traffic problems may be eased with the advent of varied forms of rapid transportation.

The inner city deterioration will be set upon by government

subsidy and by private investment and redevelopment as well. New welfare policies on the national level are expected to reduce the pull of cities as places where the poor and transients gather. The cities will become once again a place of comfortable living as well as working places for middle-class taxpayers.

The city has always been a place where ideas were developed. They have been, and are today, the centers of learning and the seedbed of change. The church in the city has never found easy existence.

When cities are small and are able to exercise a unity of community, it is reasonably easy for the church to grow. The "first" church of the small city is usually a church of some prestige and has been able to grow by natural means—simply because it is in the center of the city and it is the "first" church. Even with its natural pull and prestige, however, it very rarely has reproduced itself, but has depended upon its sister churches in outlying areas, particularly in rural areas and small-town areas for its church growth. But, if it does not reproduce itself well locally, it plays a strong part in church growth in a larger sense. Its financial stewardship undergirds the mission programs and often undertakes programs of outreach in other areas. It, and its pastor are strong supporters of denominational programs and its leaders and pastors are often the leaders in that church's denominational life.

But, as the city gets larger and larger "first" church again has an increasingly difficult time. Quite likely it is located in the inner city and suffers with the changes in the community. In this predicament of change and city growth the church itself must change. It may elect to simply change its location by moving to the fringe area of the city where many of its members have already gone. Occasionally the old city church may elect to stay and minister to the newcomers to the area. Always this is a difficult task as church growth methods must be revised and the church loses its glamorous role of being the church to which the mayor, or the aldermen, or the university president belongs.

There are two kinds of city churches really. Those particularly which are located in the smaller cities, or in those areas of the larger cities which have not as yet become quite "inner city." Then there are those which are located in the inner city. The problems of the two churches are somewhat different, although there are many problems which both types of churches share. Let us consider first those churches of the smaller cities and of the larger ones which are able to continue to grow by utilizing the methods of church growth which have been rather traditionally used. Many of these churches are using innovated methods, but as yet they have not had to change their "personality" as seriously as has the church in the inner city.

Many of these churches are growing. The Graceland Southern Baptist Church of New Albany, Indiana, is situated in a city of approximately 50,000 population. Although it is peripheral to the larger metropolitan influence of Louisville, Kentucky, it still has a very special identity of its own. The church has been in existence for approximately twelve years and in that period of time it managed to build a sanctuary that was more than adequate for years to come, accomplish an extremely slow growth throughout its history, accomplish a heavy debt to the point that it was $1,400 in arrears in payment of its current bills.

It decided to grow. The decision for growth is always sparked by some pastor with "stars in his eyes." In this case his name was Elvis Markham. The basic philosophy which was used and which was communicated to his church was:

1. That the only thing that defeats us is our attitude.
2. If we are doing what God wants done we have all the resources of God.
3. We are born to win, not to lose.
4. God has placed us here for such a time as this.
5. God is always bigger than our plans.
6. If we are concerned about a man going to hell, we are also concerned about his living in hell *now*. God calls us to minister to the total man.

The church caught the spark of his enthusiasm and set about to win a city.

In order to get the church actively involved in growth, the congregation was engaged in a study program which would help them to know how to get involved. The study program included the study of the Holy Spirit. It sought to discover the church member's talents which could be used as resources. It produced a research of the whole city of New Albany. It included a study of the ministry of prayer. In a report by Presley A. Morris, superintendent of missions for Southeastern Indiana (Southern Baptist), several exciting ideas resulted from the membership's studies which have been mentioned. Perhaps these ideas might be called objectives or purposes. They are as follows:

1. We must not just preach the gospel. We must live it.
2. A *Revolution* is needed in the church.
3. The congregation needs to provide its resources for a city-wide ministry to all races of people.
4. Every organization in the church must be directed toward evangelizing the city and meeting needs.
5. Methods utilized must be appropriate to the need.
6. Methods must be changed if needed.
7. The program must come from the needs of the people.
8. Jesus Christ must be the *Central Idea* in every program.

Many exciting things were to follow. A seminary student was called by the church to serve as a missionary to the inner city of New Albany. A house was rented in the neighborhood. The pastor moved in. There were hundreds of potential prospects but it was necessary to discover their needs and to identify the means by which the ministries would be performed. The community was surveyed and an immediate need seemed to be a children's day camp. The church used buses and simply with signs on them advertising "camp" were driven through the community offering to provide a ride to camp. At first only two boys responded, but later these spread the word and the ministry grew.

The time of meeting was Saturday morning. The place, on the

missionary's back porch. The activities consisted of singing, Bible study, recreation, refreshments. Each boy was given a New Testament. Now and then there were activities of special interest to the young people. The family of each person enlisted in the day camp were visited and the buses of the church were used to transport the people to the Graceland Church on Sundays and special occasions.

Within a few months, the number of day camps, or clubs, was enlarged to three. Some met in houses, others in yards. A beauty club was started for girls where for six weeks beauticians who were members of Graceland Church taught the girls beauty care. Later there were classes in sewing, modeling, Bible study, dramatics, and meetings where special items of interest were discussed.

A class was started for boys who were interested in mechanics. The instruction was carried on by members of the Graceland Church.

The program in the inner city soon had become so large a store-front building was rented in the inner city area. It provided a meeting place for many of the inner city activities of the church. It was given the name Alpha and Omega. Programs centering in this location were handcraft, physical recreation, Bible study, music, and many discussion groups. During the summer a day camp Bible school was conducted. A Bible fellowship class for adults was started in the community. This inner-city ministry was carried out as an intregal part of the Graceland Church. The church set about to bring people who were reached in the inner-city ministries to its worship services and other special programs in its church house. This has a tendency to integrate the people from all sections of the city and to integrate the programs of the church as well. Within a few months forty persons had made a profession of faith in the inner-city ministry and had united with the Graceland Church. Some of those who were saved have since become active leaders in the inner-city ministry.

The church discovered a need for ministry in the Bono Housing Project. It utilized a seminary student again to help in the development of this work. The program here was very similar to that conducted in the inner-city area. Persons who were enlisted in the various projects of ministry in the housing project were enlisted for the Sunday School and worship services in the Graceland sanctuary on Sunday morning. As the ministry grew, it became increasingly difficult to find a place to meet. The apartment of the seminary student or those of the persons living in the housing project were inadequate for all of the ministries that were to be performed.

Without success, the Graceland Church had tried to rent the recreational facilities of the housing project and it seemed as though the ministry would have to be curtailed. In emergency, during the summer, it had conducted Bible classes in the church buses which were parked in the vicinity of the housing project, but with the coming of cold weather it was not possible to do this. The publisher of the local newspaper, hearing of the intentions of the church, came to the rescue. It printed a story with pictures of what was taking place in the Bono Housing Project. It told of the desire of the Graceland Church to use the recreational facility for some of the ministries. A meeting at the town hall was held and the church was permitted to use the facilities.

The work of the housing project ministry however was not limited to the recreational facilities. True, there was a Sunday School and preaching service in the recreational facilities, but, in addition, there were Bible classes in homes, sewing clubs for girls, arts and crafts and Bible clubs for teen-agers. In the summertime buses were used for additional space in the project. Bus drivers carried out a visitation program in the project on Sunday morning while other members of the church taught classes in the buses.

The church worked with the housing authority in helping families who were in need. It administered a work-aid program so that people could earn money by working at the church or other places of employment. Food and clothing were distributed to those who needed them. A softball team was sponsored.

A high-rise apartment for the elderly is part of the Bono Housing Project. A ministry to the elderly was begun by a pastoral ministry to a lady who had lost a loved one. This evidence of compassion caused the people of the high rise to welcome the Graceland people. They requested a worship service to be held in their apartment. This was done and the ministry is interfaith and includes all of the love and ministry that the church can extend. These ministries include an art class, Bible classes, sewing classes, a bus trip to the state park once a year. The elderly are taken shopping and provided bus transportation to the services and elsewhere on special occasions.

The spirit of witness and ministry enlarged. The laymen of the church discovered a need in the Beechwood Housing Project and began an extension Sunday School there. Here again buses were used for Sunday School classes and became known as "rolling chapels." The buses drive in and the laymen visit in the project inviting the people to come. As many as forty people have attended the classes in the buses. Transportation is also provided to the sponsoring church on Sunday morning.

The Parkwood mission was a church-type mission located in a vast area of New Albany suburbia. A mission pastor was called to develop this mission and a house-to-house survey was made. There were 435 homes in the area. As prospects were discovered, the pastor visited them. He secured key leaders from the church who were living in the Parkwood community and conducted a training session on the nature and function of the church (the training session was held at Graceland on Sunday nights). A home fellowship Bible study was conducted in the Parkwood area. Later, Sunday School and worship services were begun in the pastor's home (and in the homes of some of the neighbors).

Soon this mission was averaging 50 in Sunday School and worship service. A building site was purchased. With the help of the Southern Baptist Convention's Home Mission Board, trailer chapels were placed on the property.

Another ministry was begun in the Green Valley section of New Albany. This area will also quite likely produce another self-supporting church. Many members of this church have been members of the mother church.

The Emmanuel Baptist Church was a church in the city of New Albany about to die. Graceland learned of her sister church's plight and offered to give assistance. The assistance was accepted and so laymen from Graceland shared their resources, both spiritual and physical, seeking to breathe life into the Emmanuel church.

In all of the studies of church growth, it is seldom seen that neighboring churches such as this give assistance to each other. As earlier mentioned, now and then in rural areas two or more churches may form a field or a parish, but it seems that so often in the city, churches are not accustomed to doing this. It is true they often will work indirectly to give assistance to a sister church in need, that is through their association, or presbytery, or some similar denominational structure, but it is relatively rare that one church directly goes to the aid of another in this way.

One of the newest ministries of the Graceland Church is a bus ministry provided to military personnel who live in the housing area of a large industrial plant which provides material for military defense. A sergeant stationed there drives the bus to transport people to Graceland on Sundays for services. The bus is also used for other purposes in the new ministry.

The results of the Graceland ministry have been many. The church which was struggling became a *serving* church. Graceland's members have rediscovered the true nature and ministry of the church. The people are *involved*. Sunday School and church attendance more than doubled in two years.

Evangelistic results have doubled. Contributions tremendously increased from an income which could not even accommodate the current bills to a 1970 budget in excess of $130,000.

One significant accomplishment is that the social strata of the congregation is fused together. Common laborers, teachers, university professors, business executives, businessmen, and others are working hand in hand (including all races) in the ministry of the church.

Other churches have been inspired and encouraged by what the Graceland church has been able to do and the city itself has been awakened to the validity of a church.

Of course there are problems involved in such a program as this. The program is time consuming and it is difficult to convince the people to become a part of the vital "dream." Real discipline is demanded in that there are many people who are prone to drop out. The church has to adjust to failure as well as success. Not all ministries will succeed, but then as the pastor says, "failure is not fatal."

It is difficult to find time for the leadership to think creatively and difficult for the congregation to become willing to break with traditions in order to accomplish a ministering performance as a church.

None of these problems can ever be overcome completely because of the humanness of church members. But then, Christ has seen fit to use persons such as this as his partner in accomplishing the growth of the Kingdom.

The First Baptist (American) Church of Monongahela, Pennsylvania, experienced a growth of 83 members in one year's time. This church was encouraged to grow through the use of Bible study, visitation, and prayer groups. The means for growth was the introduction of a bus ministry which provided transportation (and ministry) for persons who were brought to the services of the church. The young people, however, conducted summer mission programs which reached 3,000 children and produced 500 decisions for Christ in one summer. The Wednesday night "Hour of Power" has become an exciting adventure in the spiritual growth and inspiration to outreach in the church. (Report received from the pastor, Daniel Sommer.)

The First Baptist Church of Van Nuys, California, is fifty-four years old and is growing at a compound annual rate of about 15 percent. It received 773 members in a recent twelve-month period, with 425 of these new members coming by profession of faith. The average Sunday School attendance is approximately 3,000.

The method used in effecting the growth is that of involving the membership in a program of outreach to non-Christians. These are encouraged to come to the church, become involved in it and its activities, and as the church's business administrator says, "This then gives us an opportunity to preach the gospel to them."

The church utilizes all of its buildings all of the time it possibly can. It operates an active weekday program, a fully integrated Sunday School, a completely active music and choir program, and it seeks to make the church the center of social and spiritual activities in the family life.

The church has an active board of missions and attempts to promote missions in the local church through sending their young people to various parts of the country, as well as various parts of the world, and wherever possible to have an adult accompany them (at their own expense). They, too, come back on fire for missions.

They have used a radio program for their 9:30 and 11:00 A.M. services on Sunday morning. The church has 59 full-time paid employees and 76 who work part time. Lay leaders are involved in all activities of the church if possible. The church's music program is extremely active. There are 27 choir groups, 8 instrumental groups, with 1,800, plus leaders, enrolled in the music program.

A large group of young people recently made a trip to the Philippines on what is called a "Certain Sounds Outreach." (Report received from the church, prepared by Edward S. Welge, Business Administrator.)

The Travis Avenue Baptist Church of Fort Worth, Texas, is a large city church of over 6,000 members and a church property valued in excess of three million dollars. The church is made up of some professional people, such as engineers, accountants, schoolteachers, sales persons, small businessmen, and skilled workmen. The spiritual environment is conservative and it is quite aggressive in its outreach.

It uses a traditional Southern Baptist organization to help it in accomplishing its growth (approximately 500 members a year). It gives especial attention to the use of Vacation Bible Schools and to the use of church buses. Prior to the operation of Vacation Bible School, the community is canvassed to preenrol children for the school. In a recent year, over 1,500 children were enrolled in the Bible school and there were 76 professions of faith.

The church sponsors and participates in work in an inner city mission project and gives support to the Texas River Ministry.

The director of education notes that a direction toward growth is accomplished by putting an emphasis upon the results rather than upon the process or the method.

It is difficult to be adequately selective in noting the examples of church growth which are taking place in churches in the cities. Attention has been given to many such churches in earlier writings.

The growth of the First Baptist Church of Hammond, Indiana, is one of these which had phenomenal growth, as has the First Baptist Church of Dallas, Texas, and the Walnut Street Baptist Church of Louisville, Kentucky. These three churches are located in the inner city. Many other churches have died under less pressing circumstances.

A motivation to grow, however, has been seriously maintained. Because of this, methods have been devised whereby the growth was accomplished.

8 They Grow in the Inner City

Churches grow in the inner city

. . as in Philadelphia.

. . the inner city may be the most exciting "front line"

. . very seldom is the inner city church able to support itself financially

. . But it is a magnificent training ground for Christian workers who dare to test their faith.

Some are working at it in

. . Brooklyn

. . and Jacksonville, Florida

. . Dallas, Texas

and to conclude

"Do you believe God speaks to people directly?" asked the young housewife I had met through our church's telephone canvassing. We sat at the table in her small kitchen with some neighbors she had called in for the minister's visit. I said, *"God reveals himself to us directly."*

"The reason I asked," she continued, "is that we were playing with the Ouija Board, when suddenly it spelled out 'this is the Lord God speaking.' It went on to tell us some things we would do; was it really God?

While listening I sipped a cup of hot coffee and felt all my instincts rejecting her conclusions. In honesty I replied, "I couldn't deny the validity of your experience. God is unlimited in the way he reveals himself, but your experience is quite unusual."

Noting her eagerness to understand her experiences and seeing the curiosity, I explored, "Would you like to meet some evening each week and talk about your questions concerning God?"

Eyes brightened and heads nodded around the table approvingly.

This is a personal account of how a new Bible fellowship was born in the inner city of Philadelphia. The story was recounted by C. Burtt Potter, Jr., director of Inner City Ministries for Southern Baptists in Philadelphia.

The beginning of this Bible fellowship was one of 13 which Burtt Potter established in the beginning of his work. "Informal fellowships attract all kinds," Burtt said, "enthusiasts inclined toward speaking in tongues, unbelievers, Bible scholars, and Bible illiterates, emotionally starved, and those whom we would call normal."

The Bible fellowships used here seek to meet and minister to the needs of persons where they are.

"Several common purposes underlie these fellowship groups," Burtt Potter continued. "Some of these purposes are:

1. They seek to communicate the revelation of God in Jesus Christ.
2. They hope to guide unbelievers to commitment in Christ.
3. They serve to deepen the commitment of Christians to their Lord.
4. They aim at offering an open atmosphere for persons to express their feelings about God and others, so they will be able to understand and deal constructively with these feelings.
5. They seek to bridge the gap between nominal religious interest and a vital life in the church."

Burtt Potter expresses the belief that the outreach of Bible fellowship groups used in the inner city inevitably produce redemptive and healing effects in people's lives, and simultaneously, indifferent persons become related to Christ's church.

"A lonely, self-centered man who had been rejected by his church following a divorce, hadn't attended church in twelve years. After feeling comfortable with a group of Christians in a Bible fellowship, he gained a vital relationship with God, and now attends church weekly. Christianity became a commitment to Christ, rather than legalistic obedience."

In another illustration he speaks of how four young couples participated in a Bible fellowship for more than a year. They involved their neighbors in periodic participation and served as a nucleus for a chapel after eighteen months. One of the young ladies, who was a member of the church, reluctantly agreed to hold a Bible fellowship in her home at one time. After a positive response by unchurched neighbors at the initial meeting she volunteered her home again and found a deepening commitment to the church.

Potter has found that the logical approach to starting a fellowship group is for a church to sponsor such meetings in the homes of its members. The members invite prospects in the neighborhood and personal friends to participate.

When the first Bible fellowship began in Philadelphia there was only a handful of interested people. This led to the establishment of the first mission, the University Baptist Chapel. From this congregation, two fellowships emerged, one for married students and the other for single students. These groups provided the means of outreach to others on various campuses who weren't involved in the life of the church. A variety of approaches have been used in this inner-city ministry in Philadelphia. These include:

1. Door-to-door visitation.
2. Distribution of leaflets in mailboxes of apartment houses.
3. Telephone canvassing to provide multiple ministries to interested persons.
4. Interpersonal relationships through which friends were invited to participate.
5. Contacting and grouping persons according to common interest, age, or background.

The subject matter used by the groups was determined by the needs and interests of the groups, the purpose, knowledge, capability, and resources of the leader. Some groups began discussing their immediate ethical or social problems and focused on the biblical revelation for the answers. Other groups chose to use special Bible study materials. The thirteen week undated doctrinal curriculum, provided by the Sunday School Board of the Southern Baptist Convention for Bible fellowships, was found to be valuable.

Most of the groups began studying a book of the New Testament in a modern translation. The Gospels were found to be a starting place for immature Christians and unbelievers. More mature Christians preferred weighter discussions from the Epistles.

The duration of the group's existence depended upon the purpose of its creation. Some of the groups lasted for six weeks, some lasted as much as eighteen weeks.

If the group's purpose was to form personal relationships with unchurched persons that could be cultivated into the full fellowship of the church, the fellowship might last as much as six months to a year.

If the purpose was primarily educational, with the intention of presenting a specific curriculum, the task was accomplished in a shorter period of time.

If the sense of "groupness" began to wane and evidences of growth within the members was not apparent, the participants simply concluded the fellowship.

The dynamics of the group atmosphere and the content of the Bible teaching provided ingredients for transformation within individuals and effectiveness in church outreach.

Another approach that was utilized (without the benefit of a formal building) was that of holding Bible classes in backyards and neighborhood parks. Let the pastor tell that story.

"We originally intended to hold four Vacation Bible Schools in various sections of the city that seemed right for starting new chapels. There was only one Southern Baptist mission in Philadelphia at the time that could sponsor these efforts for outreach in unknown neighborhoods. Summer missionaries who had been sent as a part of the Student Summer Mission program of the Southern Baptist Convention and volunteers from suburban churches were the workers for the projected endeavor.

"It was in the summer that two summer missionaries canvassed 1,500 homes in a middle-income white community. After spending a week in distributing invitations to the children to attend our Vacation Bible School, we anticipated an exciting Monday. We waited and waited and not a single child came.

"We were heartbroken! We had secured the backyard of a twin home and had tape-recorded music. We had handwork ready, our program formed, and there was not a child in sight."

"A friend who was present reminded us that several years ago in Absecon, New Jersey, they had modified a Vacation Bible School approach and emphasized the recreational aspect to draw the young people.

"We determined to do the same. The summer workers went into another similar community. There was only one close friend we knew in this area and she volunteered her yard. By the end of the week the canvassers saw a different response to their invitation to a neighborhood recreation program. They predicted over a hundred children to be present on Monday.

"I approached the only other Protestant lady I knew in the area and asked if she would allow us to use her backyard too. She hesitated, but her husband agreed. Providentially, five other backyards were later volunteered for on a bright Monday morning 140 children gathered in front of the house to enrol. By the end of the week there were over 160 children, between three and twelve years of age involved.

"The lady who had been reluctant to let us use her yard became most interested in the program and was sitting on the ground by Wednesday helping juniors assemble 'treasure chests' with popsicle sticks.

"Two principal purposes are expressed for these activities. They are (1) to explore and cultivate a neighborhood for the purpose of establishing a mission, and (2) to cultivate relationships with the young people that will succeed in channeling them to some vital area of church life."

Many people have made Christian decisions as the result of

these programs whereby vital information is transmitted. And, of course, there is an influence upon the parents of the children who become receptive to those who work with their offspring. Pastor Potter observes that in communities that are predominately Protestant Bible class activities are successful by any name. It is in communities that are principally unchurched that neighborhood recreation programs make the difference between success and failure. These programs have been sponsored in Negro ghettos at times when the racial mood was tense and upon one occasion over 80 black children attended. They and their parents requested that the workers come back for a second week. Low-income white communities and affluent communities have seen equal success. In integrated sections of the city there have been as many as 80 involved in one week's program.

The first on the program is the Bible story, while the children are relaxed and susceptible to learning. This lasts about twenty minutes.

The second activity is supervised recreation, such as relay races, dodge ball, etc.

Then there is refreshment time, followed by periods for crafts.

Dropouts are virtually unknown. The relaxed structure of the schedule enables the church workers to establish lasting relationships.

The average cost of providing free refreshments and crafts to the children is thirty-seven cents per child per week.

Of course there is a problem involved in securing workers for such a program. Older teen-agers are often used, along with adult faculty members. If possible, the pastor suggests several churches could cooperate in such an endeavor.

Home fellowship Bible classes and neighborhood programs were not the only techniques used for building a witness in Philadelphia's inner city. These activities were carried on without a building in which the congregation could meet. It became increasingly important that the beginning congregation find a center of activities.

Ultimately, an abandoned church house was located and purchased in the inner city. A denomination which was friendly toward the work which Pastor Potter was seeking to carry on owned the church house and for several reasons were not able to keep it open. They agreed to sell the building for $10,000, a ridiculously small sum of money for such a large building. The new congregation, with the help of many neighbors, set about to renovate the old church house. Many years of grime and dirt were removed. New paint, gutters, and in some instances, roofing were applied.

Now with the building it was possible to carry on a regular Sunday morning program. Weekday ministries of various kinds were instituted. Recreational programs were carried on for the children after school. Church organizations were established, including missionary organizations for adults and young people. In January of 1971, fifty people made Christian decisions in the church. Most of these were upon profession of faith.

The effect of the church in the inner city was, as expected to be, one of reconciliation. At one time, in the beginning of the services, it seemed that it would be impossible because of vandalism and undisciplined behavior of the children to continue the work. But, through examples of love and patience, reconciliation came. Churches can grow in the inner city!

In fact, it may well be that the inner city may be the most exciting front line of Christian growth. Certainly it is no place for lazy church members. Nor, is it a place for Christians of low-level commitment. Traditional approaches of church growth which may have been more successfully used in the suburbs, the small cities, small towns, or rural areas are often found not to be so successful in the inner city.

The inner cities, however, are the areas of some of our greatest needs. These areas contain the ghettos and often the very affluent in high-rise apartments. The depraved, the disillusioned, the lonely often live here.

The inner city church is very seldom able to support itself.

Its success is most likely dependent upon the largess of Christian giving of suburban churches and other churches outside the inner city area.

Christian ministry in the inner city provides a magnificent training ground for the Christian worker who dares to test his faith.

The South Third Street United Methodist Church of Brooklyn, New York, operates the "Anchor House" in the inner city of Brooklyn. Several years ago, in response to a need, it started a drug addiction rehabilitation program which was later moved to 976 Park Place where the Mission Board purchased a house (to be known as the "Anchor House"). Drug addiction seemed to be the biggest problem in the area. The church started a Spanish language telephone ministry. Through this it used the opportunity of speaking to those who needed counseling, sometimes desperately.

The Anchor House which is operated from the South Third Street United Methodist Church, is in reality a "half-way house for the rehabilitation of drug addicts."

The Main Street (Southern) Baptist Church of Jacksonville, Florida, is a church which is over sixty years old. It is a downtown church in a transitional area which is fast becoming a low income level community with many apartments. This area is characterized by the usual number of "rent hoppers." The community is also changing on racial grounds. It was once an all white neighborhood which is now integrated. In some areas the whites have remained and others the whites have moved out creating a Negro community. The educational level of the children in the community is basically low.

The church rebuilt its sanctuary five years ago and it also built an educational plant and remodeled another. The total cost of all the buildings is approximately one million dollars. The church debt is fantastic and has been one factor that has hindered the outreach program. However, the church is growing, and showed an actual increase in its membership of 2,163 to a membership of approximately 2,400 in 1970.

The church is made up of many older members who demonstrated a traditional type of faith, however, they are the very "backbone" of the church. It is amazing how the retired recipients of Social Security readily give one tenth of their income to support the church. It is this determination on the part of the membership that has kept the church growing. They are determined that the church will live and grow.

The church carries on an active mission program through its organizations, particularly the Woman's Missionary Union and the Mission Action Groups. The church operates a weekday ministry and a program for the youth of the community.

One particular program that had remarkable effect upon the membership was one launched by the pastor which was called "claim a block for Christ." On a particular Sunday morning the pastor asked those who would be willing to serve as a "home missionary" and be responsible for ministering to a block in the community, to commit themselves. Over one hundred people agreed to accept this responsibility and were assigned a block for community visitation. This visitation was not directed primarily toward church membership, but to discover the needs of the people and to devise means of following up in meeting the needs. The Christian Social Ministry committee of the church made a survey of the community to discover what agencies and institutions were available as resources to meet the needs of the people. It was discovered that there were many such agencies and that these were provided to assist the church and be assisted by the church. Some of these agencies already in existence in the community which were discovered was a nondenominational Bible club located in the Boys Club. A local school was willing to place a class for basic adult education in the church. Vocation rehabilitation was willing to refer families in spiritual need to the church. The local justice of the peace referred nonreaders to the church; church members taught them how to read. Tutorial services for elementary children was a possibility and it was discovered that there was no agency or institutional program to care for the needs of young girls. As a result of this study, many new opportunities of service were opened. The church planned to develop a program for girls, adult education, and for senior citizens.

The Hampton Place Baptist (Southern) Church of Dallas, Texas, is a church forty years old in a changing community (from largely Anglo-Saxon to 20 percent Latin). The houses in the community are in the $6,000 to $18,000 bracket and the community is declining. Over one half of the membership lives at least two miles away. The Sunday School enrolment in 1964 was 1,505. In 1969, it was 2,061. Additions to the church in the five-year period were 1,678. But because of the high transiency of the community the membership increased from 2,226 to 2,911. What is the major method utilized in accomplishing such exciting growth? One of the answers is the weekly visitation program which averages 160 participants.

The Woman's Mission Action Groups are given much of the credit for keeping alive and aggressive a philosophy for local mission action.

The church growth is strongly structured. There are 40 active committees. There is a tremendous emphasis upon Christian training (with the largest numbers of members receiving training awards of any church in the Southern Baptist Convention).

Increased public relations is credited with providing much assistance. The use of radio and newspaper advertisements, yard signs, direct mail, a weekly newspaper, and billboards have called attention to the ministry of the church. The church utilizes special youth groups, music groups, drama, apartment programs, and other special programs in the area of recreation to provide enlarging contacts.

Although this is not typically an inner-city church, it is a church in a changing community and therefore suffers many of the problems of the inner-city church.

Conclusion

Where then do churches grow? There are examples from all across America. The growth has occurred to churches which are large, and churches which are small.

There are several things which have typified them, as we have noticed their growth.

1. They are churches with a purpose. They know what "church" is all about, whether that definition agrees with everyone's definition is not so important as the fact that the churches do have a purpose. Its purpose is to live in the name of Christ.
2. The church has a leadership which speaks with authority. These leaders would sometimes engender criticisms from others who observed. Some would say to them that they were concerned about their personal image and in what church growth would mean to them in their religious, political orbits. The criticism is unjust. God's people who lead well have been able to speak with authority. They have been able to speak with authority because they had confidence in the truths about which they spoke. There were no uncertain trumpets.
3. Not only have the churches which have grown had a purpose and their leadership spoken with authority, but the church and its leadership together has developed a strategy for growth. They intended to grow. This strategy for growth has taken many forms. In the illustrations which have been used it is noted that nearly all methods of church growth have been utilized by some churches in the open country, small town, small city, suburban area, and in the inner city. But, not all churches use all forms. Successful growing churches were selective in the forms which they used and made them applicable in the community where they existed.
4. Churches which are growing know their communities. They have devised special means of discovering needs in their

communities. Whether that simply meant a well developed sensitivity to the community needs, or whether it was a formalized door-to-door canvas of the community, the church discovered community needs and sought to meet the needs.

5. This has called for involvement. People involvement. No church which is really growing has relegated its responsibility to hired hands. It is true the churches have utilized church staff in accordance with the size of the congregation and in accordance with resources of the church to supply specialized staff. But the job has not been left up to the staff. The church staff has been used in equipping roles to help lay people become involved in the growth of the church.
6. Church growth takes many forms. Some growth is immediate; other is designed for future harvests. Some manifests itself in a deepened spiritual life within the church. Some is evidenced in the changed lives of those newly won to Christ.

Over 200 churches were studied. Many of these which were not included here could well have been included. In those churches which were studied, it did not seem to be important how rich or poor, how learned or unlettered—with the right motivation, with dedication, commitment, sensitivity to the community and its needs, and the willingness to become involved in the lives of people, they grow.

CHURCHES CAN GROW!

AND NOW . . . FINALLY

One of the pastors wrote in. He had been serving as pastor of a church in the New York City area. There was a church house in Brooklyn. He wondered if we would buy it. The community was teeming with children, people of many nationalities. It was a decaying community. A pall of tension hung over it. There were riots, drug addicts and alcoholics, and just lonely people. Would we be willing to buy the house?

He enclosed a picture. He described the congregation which once had used this facility. The picture revealed a mighty edifice, once endowed with magnificent stained-glass windows. It had an ornately carved door. It was surrounded by a high wrought iron fence. But even from the photograph it gave an impression of a ruin.

Who had been the congregation which once had dwelt within this mighty pile? Who first had brought the witness to this place? What had the church been like? Some itinerant merchantman may once have come to visit on this block. He had journeyed here from another town. Perhaps he had ridden out to the suburb, which once this place was, but now had ceased to be. He stopped his carriage and a friend had met him there.

He told him the *good news.* The good news that "unto us a child is born, unto us a son is given and his name shall be called Wonderful, Counselor, Almighty God, Everlasting Father, Prince of Peace." He told him—one friend told the other—that Christ was in his life come new and he was not willing that anyone would perish.

Now there were two. And "wherever there are as many as two or three gathered together . . ." there was a church. And the church in Brooklyn would never be more a church than it was in that very moment, giver and receiver of a witness. The two men went into the house. One man witnessed to his wife, soon now there were three. The church began to grow. It met in a house, or maybe it was a store-front building and the church continued to grow. It knew its community, it knew its needs, it sought to minister to them. In times of great distress, sacrificially it gave. It was not afraid. It was not intimidated by its world, by its community, or the changes in it. It was a city of refuge. It was a good place to be.

As it continued to grow it found one place then another for its meeting places. Finally, a building committee was dispatched to find a choice lot and ultimately they built it there. Magnificent heap of stone and brick and mortar and stained glass and auditorium and pipe organ! The congregation swelled inside its doors on Sunday. Large carriages drew up and disgorged the faithful to be engulfed within this huge carved door. Sounds of singing could be heard out in the streets. The prominent pastor preached a sound dogma to those who eagerly heard.

Some have said that a president of the United States once had been a member there.

But there now is a sign *for sale* fastened to the wrought iron fence. Why?

The invaders came. Did they mount their catapults to throw their armaments against the wall? No, not in this day. Who were they who came? They were stalking invaders from some "foreign" place like Italy or Poland or Puerto Rico or Georgia. And they moved in the houses on the block. They were no heathen horde who came. They knew Christ in their lands too. And having moved on this block met the fortress face to face. Great pile of stone, bearing high a cross pointing skyward to the face of God, and with a wrought iron fence around its base.

Wrought iron fence?

Who built it there?

Who first devised the means of keeping the world from out the church. To protect the church, some devoted follower had said, "We must protect the church from the world." "People with strange languages and strange ways of life threaten our fellowship. We must be protected from the world."

And so they built the fence.

And an usher was stationed at the gate to admit "members only."

And so, it died. But such a church which would protect itself from the world discovers that churches do not live by that which they hold to themselves. Certainly they do not grow. The secret in living cannot be contained behind a fence. Churches grow only in proportion to how they give themselves away, and if they refuse, then all they have is taken.

Protected from the world? No, the wrought iron fence couldn't do it.

The world came to hate the fence and those who erected it—who said, "We love you," but shouted all of its "I love you's" from behind the fence.

The wall was broken down.

The horde that was the world about it (really no more than the people of its own community) broke down the gates and stormed the doors. They broke the panes of stained glass in the windows and scribed their obscenities around the wall of what had been a sanctuary.

What was it like inside?

As I looked at the photograph, I wondered. I imagined the vaulted ceilings climbing up from well-carved colonnades. I imagined the pews in disarray. The damp smell of long disuse.

My ears heard the echoes of great sermons preached from the chancel there. Great dogmas, sound doctrines.

A Bible's leaf blew through the long dry baptistry.

Someone said, "See Joe, see where the Christians were?"

M. W. B.